Deschutes
Public Library

THE GREAT GENERALS SERIES

This distinguished new series features the lives of eminent military leaders who changed history in the United States and abroad. Top military historians write concise but comprehensive biographies including the personal lives, battles, strategies, and legacies of these great generals, with the aim to provide background and insight into today's armies and wars. These books are of interest to the military history buff, and, thanks to fast-paced narratives and references to current affairs, they are also accessible to the general reader.

Patton by Alan Axelrod

Grant by John Mosier

Eisenhower by John Wukovits

LeMay by Barrett Tillman

MacArthur by Richard B. Frank

Stonewall Jackson by Donald A. Davis

Bradley by Alan Axelrod

Pershing by Jim Lacey

Andrew Jackson by Robert V. Remini

Sherman by Steven E. Woodworth

Lee by Noah Andre Trudeau

Marshall by H. Paul Jeffers

Grant

GRANT
Copyright © John Mosier, 2006.
All rights reserved.

First published in hardcover in 2006 by St. Martin's Griffin in
the US–a division of St. Martin's Press LLC, 175 Fifth Avenue, New York,
NY 10010.

St. Martin's Griffin are registered trademarks in the United States,
the United Kingdom, Europe and other countries.

ISBN-13: 978-0-230-61393-5
ISBN-10: 0-230-61393-4

Library of Congress Cataloging-in-Publication Data
Mosier, John, 1944–
    Grant/John Mosier.
        p.   cm.—(Great Generals)
    Includes bibliographical references and index
    ISBN 1-4039-7136-6 (cloth)
    ISBN 0-230-61393-4 (paperback)
    1. Grant, Ulysses S. (Ulysses Simpson), 1822–1885.   2. Grant, Ulysses
S. (Ulysses Simpson), 1822–1885—Military leadership.   3. Generals—
United States—Biography.   4. United States. Army—Biography.
5. Command of troops—History—19th century.   6. Strategy—
History—19th century.   7. Presidents—United States—Biography.
I. Title   II. Series
E672.M67   2006
973.8'2092—dc22
[B]

                                                            2005056370

A catalogue record of the book is available from the British Library.

Design by Letra Libre

First St. Martin's Griffin paperback edition: January 2009
P1

Grant

John Mosier

ST. MARTIN'S GRIFFIN ☙ NEW YORK

Contents

Photosection appears between pages 100 and 101

Foreword

GRANT WAS THE GENERAL WHOSE STRATEGIC BRILLIANCE, tactical acumen, and courage won the Civil War for the Union. But, more than any other, he is the source for the war-winning ways of the modern American armed forces.

Grant's is the real American story. Mid-American in his roots and undistinguished in appearance, from a successful but not wealthy family, his search for an affordable higher education led to a commission as a lieutenant in the US Army. After his graduation from West Point he served as a junior officer in combat in the expeditionary force in Mexico. He was fortunate to see both battle and the logistics behind it, and then, unable to adequately support his family through a peacetime Army career, he left the military and sought his future in civilian life. As told by John Mosier, the story of how this seemingly ordinary man forever changed his country and our world is compelling in its urgency and profound in its significance. Start with his talents—despite an apparently undistinguished academic record, Grant possessed unusual gifts. He was a natural in mathematics, having taught himself algebra and possessing an uncanny memory for numbers. He was a voracious reader with wide-ranging interests. He had strong skills in drawing and painting, with a keen eye for details. He possessed a strong physical constitution with outstanding endurance. And he had an unusual temperament: self-contained, focused, and unflappable. He had a strong, practical intelligence. His soldiers, commanders and adversaries were all soon to learn how all this added up. In the first place, Grant thought through problems. He had a restless, but patient mind and he brought to the solutions not only his fine attention to detail but a compelling grasp of time-space relationships. He seemed to always know where he was, what he could do with his own forces, and what his adversaries could do to him. Today, we might call this situational awareness. All this led to a superior ability to think ahead of events, what the Soviets later came to call "foresight." But if that were all he had, he'd have been no more than an outstanding staff aide, critiquing the battle afterwards, or tugging on the general's sleeve to offer suggestions. No, Grant had a way about him that enabled him to transform his ideas into action through others. He had leadership. His manner bespoke authority and compelled respect in war. It was his brevity, his economy of language, his understanding of his troops, his inner confidence, his outward courage, and his implacable determination which gave his particular intellectual gifts the power to move men and shape the course of history.

Talent, and particularly military talent, is sometimes not obvious in younger officers in a peacetime army. Grant was too junior—he was almost right out of West Point—in the Mexican War to earn much recognition and he suffered in the wholesale expansion of the Union force at the beginning of the Civil War where he was one veteran among hundreds of ambitious volunteers. It was the subsequent confusion, battlefield failures, and desperate search for leadership that brought Grant's talents to public appreciation. It is Grant's rise to the top through demonstrated brilliance on the battlefield that Mosier so well describes in this book. The breadth of Grant's incredible talent was this: he was both a brilliant battlefield commander and, as his responsibilities grew, a brilliant strategic commander. By his personal command he was a decisive force in battle, while steering the strategic maneuver of armies hundreds of miles distant, he ultimately crushed the opposing state, the confederacy. Grant had an uncanny way of being present at the decisive point in battle no matter the personal risk. He had unerringly assembled the maneuvers in battles to seize strategic victory. No one else in American history has quite done this—not Patton, nor Eisenhower, not Pershing, not Lee. Washington was closest, but without the compression of events caused by telegraphic communications and railroads.

The Union forces were committed to reconstruction and demobilized after the war. The civilian volunteers largely returned to their private lives, and the regimental colors were furled. Only a shadow of the great force remained thirty years later. Nevertheless, Grant's leadership was transformative in shaping our Army over the next century and a half, for Grant taught us how to fight: take on the enemy, and don't let go. Don't philosophize or intellectualize. Defeat the enemy force in battle. Use all arms and all means. Match innovation with common sense. Treat the defeated enemy with respect. And in Grant's character and conduct, thousands of leaders have found guidance and a model for our own behavior. His stoic, imperturbable command on the battlefield is the aim of every commander as was his moral courage, patience, and dogged, quiet loyalty to his chain of command, despite the political machinations ambitious fellow officers. His basic, common decency and respect for others represent the essential starting point for effective leadership in a democratic society. These are the character traits most prized, and most respected in the American Armed Forces today.

In 1991, then-US Army Chief of Staff General Gordon Sullivan grounded his corps of Army generals in the character of Grant, when he gave to many of us a pocket-knife. The blade was inscribed "Sherman to Grant" in reference to General Sherman's famous tribute to Grant's leadership after the battle of Shiloh: "I knew where ever I was that you thought of me, and if I got in a tight place, you would come, if alive.". For it was that bond between soldiers, from Privates to Generals, that Grant gave us. Above all, Grant had the unique combination of almost instinctive common sense in battle and superior strategic vision without which Union victory might never have been achieved. It is to that elusive combination which every program of military leadership development ultimately aims, whether in the United States or elsewhere. It's a good recipe for success in business, and in life, too. And all this from an "ordinary man" from the mid-west—a true American hero and one of history's greatest Captains.

—*General Wesley K. Clark*

Who's Who in *Grant*

Nathaniel Banks: Union general who was commander of the Department of the Gulf when Grant was trying to capture Vicksburg.

P.G.T. Beauregard: Confederate army general who fought at the First Battle of Bull Run; he assumed command of Confederate forces at the Battle of Shiloh after Johnston's death.

Braxton Bragg: Confederate general and commander of the Army of Tennessee who participated in the Battle of Shiloh; he was defeated by Grant at Chattanooga.

James Buchanan: Fifteenth president of the United States and Lincoln's predecessor.

Simon B. Buckner: Confederate general and pre-War friend of Grant who surrendered command at the Battle of Fort Donelson.

Don Carlos Buell: Brigadier general of the Union Army and head of the Department of the Ohio for operations in eastern Tennessee; he participated in the battle of Shiloh.

Ambrose E. Burnside: Union commander of the Army of the Potomac; he later became general of all Union armies.

Sylvanus Cadwallader: Journalist who covered the Union side of the Civil War.

Jefferson Davis: President of the Confederate States and commander of the Confederate Army.

Earl van Dorn: Confederate cavalry commander; he fought Grant in Mississippi.

John B. Floyd: U.S. Secretary of War, and senior Confederate general at the battle for Forts Henry and Donelson.

Andrew Hull Foote: Union naval officer who led riverboats during Grant's attack on Forts Henry and Donelson.

Nathan Bedford Forrest: Confederate cavalry officer and later general who fought Grant at Fort Donelson and at the Battle of Shiloh.

Frederick the Great: King of Prussia from 1740–1786 and esteemed military commander who fought many wars; he is admired as one of the greatest tactical geniuses of all time.

John C. Frémont: An explorer, he served as a major general and headed the Department of the West during the Civil War.

Benjamin Grierson: Union cavalry commander ordered by Grant to lead a major diversionary raid deep into the Confederacy as part of the Vicksburg Campaign.

Henry W. Halleck: Union commander in chief and chief of staff; he was Grant's commander in St. Louis.

William Joseph Hardee: Confederate General who commanded a corps at the battle of Shiloh.

Thomas Harris: Confederate officer who was pursued by Grant during the early part of the war in Missouri.

Adolphus Heiman: Architect and Confederate colonel; he directed construction on the fort that would bear his name.

Ethan Allen Hitchcock: Veteran of the war of 1812 and major general in the Union Army who became special advisor to the Secretary of War during the Civil War.

John Bell Hood: Confederate General who lost every major battle while in command of the Army of Tennessee.

Joseph Hooker: Union General who lost command of the Army of the Potomac after his defeat at Fredericksburg; he fought under Grant in the Battle of Chattanooga.

Stephen A Hurlbut: Union commander of the Army of the Gulf; he served as one of Grant's divisional commanders during the Vicksburg Campaign.

Joseph Joffre: French General and commander in chief of the French Army who became famous for retreating and then counterattacking at the First Battle of the Marne in WWI.

Albert Sidney Johnston: Commander of the U.S. Army Department of the Pacific in California at the outbreak of the Civil War; he was killed in action at Shiloh as Commander of the western Confederacy.

Joseph Johnston: Confederate General who, with John Pemberton, fought Grant at the Battle of Vicksburg.

Robert E. Lee: Confederate general and general-in-chief of Confederate forces.

Abraham Lincoln: President and commander in chief of the Union forces.

John Alexander "Black Jack" Logan: Union general who served under Grant in the Western Theater; he fought at the Battle of Belmont and was wounded at Fort Donelson.

James Longstreet: A close friend of Grant before the War, he became a Confederate general who fought at the first and second Battles of Bull Run.

Nathaniel Lyon: First Union general to be killed in the Civil War; he was badly outnumbered by the Confederates at the Battle of Wilson's Creek.

George C. Marshall: Military leader and Secretary of State; he was best remembered for his role as military commander of all U.S. forces during WWII and for his work in establishing the post-war reconstruction effort for Europe, the Marshall Plan.

George McClellan: Union general and briefly the commander of the Union Army.

John A. McClernand: Lawyer, newspaper editor and congressman; he became a brigadier general during the Civil War. He was second in command under Grant at the Battle of Belmont.

George Gordon Meade: Union general and commander of the Army of the Potomac under Grant; he commanded Union forces at Gettysburg.

Helmuth von Moltke the Elder: Prussian field marshal; he led the Prussian army to victory in three successive wars and wrote noteworthy books on tactics, including *The Franco-German War of 1870–71.*

Bernard Montgomery: British general who served in India and in both world wars. He defeated Rommel in North Africa and served as British Commander under Eisenhower.

William Nelson: Navy officer and Union general who commanded the army of Kentucky, fought with Grant at Shiloh and Corinth.

John C. Pemberton: Confederate General who, with Joseph Johnston, fought Grant at the Battle of Vicksburg.

John J. Pershing: Commander in Chief of the American Expeditionary Force in WWI and General of the Armies; he was regarded as a mentor by American generals in WWII.

John Pope: Union General who headed the Army of Virginia and fought in the Second Battle of Bull Run.

Sterling Price: Confederate major general who won the Battle of Wilson's Creek and faced Grant at Corinth.

Winfield Scott: Union commander at the start of the war.

Philip Henry Sheridan: Union general assigned by Grant to command the Cavalry Corps of the Army of the Potomac.

William T. Sherman: Union general who fought as a division commander under Grant at the Battle of Shiloh and at Vicksburg. He commanded the Army of the Tennessee and was appointed by Grant as the head of the Military Division of the Mississippi.

Charles F. Smith: Union officer who eventually became a division commander in the Department of the Missouri under Grant.

Kirby Smith: Confederate General who took command of the Trans-Mississippi Department of the Confederacy after the fall of Vicksburg.

Zachary Taylor: Twelfth President of the United States; he was Grant's commander in Mexico.

George Henry Thomas: Union general who fought as a Division commander under Grant at Shiloh; he was defeated by the Confederates at Nashville.

Lloyd Tilghman: Railroad construction engineer and one of three Confederate generals in charge of Forts Henry and Donelson.

Lew Wallace: Union division commander who fought under Grant at the Battle of Fort Donelson and at Shiloh.

Elihu Washburne: Republican congressman and friend of Abraham Lincoln who supported Grant throughout his career.

Gideon Welles: United States Secretary of the Navy; his dedication to naval blockades was one of the key reasons for the North's victory over the South.

Arthur Wellesley, Duke of Wellington: Commander of the British Army in Spain during the Napoleonic wars; he defeated Napoleon at Waterloo.

Important Battles and Dates in Grant's Career

April 27, 1822   Hiram Ulysses Grant born, Point Pleasant, Ohio

September 30, 1843   Ulysses Simpson Grant graduates West Point, joins Fourth Infantry Regiment, Saint Louis, Missouri

May 7, 1844   Fourth Infantry ordered to western Louisiana

Mexican War

April 25, 1846   Hostilities begin

May 8, 1846   **Battle of Palo Alto, Texas**

May 9, 1846   **Battle of Resaca de Palma, Mexico**

September 19–25, 1846   **Battle of Monterrey, Mexico**

March 9, 1847   Winfield Scott Expedition lands in Vera Cruz

April 18, 1847   Battle of Cerro Gordo

August 20, 1847   Battle of Churubusco

September 8–13, 1847   Battles for Mexico City (Chapultepec, Molino del Rey, San Cosme)

September 14, 1847   American forces occupy Mexico City

February 2, 1848   Treaty of Guadalupe Hidalgo

Civil War

June 11, 1861	Grant appointed Colonel, 21st Illinois Volunteers
July 21, 1861	Battle of First Manassas (Bull Run)
August 7 (May 17), 1861	Grant appointed Brigadier General of Volunteers
August 29, 1861	Grant appointed to command District of South-East Missouri
November 7, 1861	**Raid on Belmont, Missouri**
February 6, 1862	**Siege and Capture of Fort Henry, Tennessee**
February 13–16, 1862	**Siege and Capture of Fort Donelson, Tennessee**
February 16, 1862	Grant promoted to Major General of Volunteers
April 6–7, 1862	**Battle of Shiloh, Tennessee**
August 29–30, 1862	Battle of Second Manassas (Bull Run)
September 17, 1862	Battle of Antietam (Sharpsburg), Maryland
September 19, 1862	**Battle of Iuka, Mississippi**
October 3–4, 1863	**Battle of Corinth, Mississippi**
December 29–30, 1862	**Battle of Chickasaw Bluffs (Vicksburg), Mississippi**
December 31, 1862	Battle of Stones River (Murfreesboro), Tennessee
May 16, 1863	Battle of Champion Hill, Mississippi
May 19-July 3, 1863	**Siege of Vicksburg**
July 1–3, 1863	Battle of Gettysburg, Pennsylvania
July 4, 1863	**Vicksburg, Mississippi, Surrenders**
July 4, 1863	Grant promoted to Major General, U. S. Army
May 1–4, 1863	Battle of Chancellorsville, Virginia
September 19–20, 1863	Battle of Chickamauga, Tennessee
October 28, 1863	**Battle of Chattanooga**
Mar 2, 1862	Grant promoted to Lieutenant General, U. S. Army

May 5–7, 1864	**Battle of the Wilderness, Virginia**
May 8–19, 1864	**Battle of Spotsylvania, Virginia**
June 14–18, 1864	**Battle of Petersburg**
September 2, 1864	Fall of Atlanta, Georgia
December 15, 1863	Battle of Nashville
April 9, 1865	Lee surrenders at Appomattox Court House, Virginia
July 25, 1866	Grant promoted to General, United States Army

*Engagements in which Grant participated or commanded in **bold**

Introduction

THERE ARE ENOUGH BIOGRAPHIES OF ULYSSES S. GRANT to fill a small library, and three of our most distinguished military historians have written accounts of his military career. In military history, Grant is an important figure. To the general reader, however, he is less known, and his considerable accomplishments on the battlefield are obscured by the specialist treatments that constitute the standard discourse of military historians.

The aim of this book is to give the general reader an understanding of Grant's generalship, and not his presidency. The portrait of Grant that this book draws differs from other biographies in many important ways.

First, the focus of this biography is on Grant the general, his strategy and legacy. For this reason, this biography is not limited to the Civil War, American history, and American generals. Grant was a world-class strategist whose achievements left a lasting imprint on the American military, and his unbroken string of victories makes him unique. The best way to understand his achievements is to compare him with his peers and heirs: the other great captains of the eighteenth and nineteenth centuries, and the modern U.S. army.

This approach involves comparisons with men whose achievements lie outside of the normal scope of American history. However, even without any knowledge of the particulars of Frederick the Great of Prussia (for example), the mere fact that the comparison can be made helps to explain Grant's importance as a general.

Most Americans have an idea about the reputation of the German army: we fought them in two wars. The founder of that army was Frederick the Great, who ruled Prussia from 1740 to 1786, turning it into a great military power. The victorious Prussian army that Frederick created and led became the model for all future German armies. So too with the army that Grant led to victory in 1865; Grant demonstrated that an army of civilians could become the best fighting force in the world, as indeed the American army has become.

Unlike many of his contemporaries, Grant did not try to establish himself as a military theorist or intellectual. But his achievements resonate with Napoleonic maxims, the first and most important being this: "In War, delay is fatal." Few if any of the other Union generals grasped that point, but Grant did. Similarly, his solutions to military problems track the solutions of Wellington and von Moltke—the two most successful generals of their times. He absorbed the basic Napoleonic ideas, and he proved himself able to direct enormous armies on a Napoleonic scale. Indeed, his abilities in this regard greatly exceeded Napoleon's, whose far-flung legions generally floundered, without the emperor's personal direction.

Both Napoleon and Frederick the Great were monarchs. The former was a despot, the latter a dictator. Like Napoleon's nemesis, the Duke of Wellington, the man who decisively beat him at Waterloo in June 1815, Grant was not only the product of a democracy, but he was deeply committed to the principles on which it was based. Grant's triumphs, then, demonstrate a point often neglected in studies of great generals. Democracies can indeed produce men who can achieve brilliant victories over formidable adversaries, men who also resist the temptation to use the power those victories give them to seek control of the state.

Grant, like Wellington and Dwight Eisenhower, was voted into high office by a citizenry that had a clear sense that this was a man who was not just a great leader, but also personified the best ideals of representative democracy. Grant thus exemplifies a tradition that is alive and well in the twenty-first century in the United States: generals who want to become the leaders of their country must run for office like everyone else.

Grant and Wellington, like Eisenhower in modern times, were morally superior to their counterparts: each was content to lead their country's armies, following the direction of the civilian administration, even though this direction was often muddled and confused.

By the end of 1863, Grant was one of the most respected and popular men in American life and his victories on the battlefield resulted in his name being brought forward as a presidential candidate. (His overwhelming victories in the 1868 and 1872 presidential elections make clear that the talk was hardly casual speculation.) General George McClellan, former commander of the main Union forces, was assiduously cultivating the Democratic party, and ultimately emerged as their candidate for the 1864 presidential election. Lincoln realized this was an election he might well lose; he was greatly relieved to learn that Grant had no intentions of letting himself be put forward in the middle of a war in which he was increasingly being seen as the Union's best hope for victory.

+≡≡≡+

In most histories of the Civil War, it is assumed that this conflict was the first modern war. Properly defined, it was not. It was, however, the last war in which Napoleon's maxim that "in war the general is everything, the mass is nothing," may fairly be said to hold. By 1870, the general staff system that had been percolating in Prussia for half a century finally came to fruition, and from then on, supreme commanders had a different function.

After the Civil War, the function of a senior general changed. Like Helmuth von Moltke the Elder, who led the Prussian armies to victory in three successive wars (Denmark, 1864; Austria, 1866; France, 1870), military leaders after Grant were administrators and strategists, and rarely if ever would even see the battlefield, much less direct combat operations.

So the Civil War was a conflict in which the radically new and modern would be blended with the traditional, thus posing an unusual challenge for any general. In 1861, as in 1815, a great captain still often had to lead from his horse, take personal control of the battle. At first Grant did so, but it is a measure of his genius that he saw that age coming to an end, and moved effortlessly from commanding an army of a few divisions to commanding no less than a dozen widely spread armies.

But a great part of Grant's genius was that he adapted his leadership to the changes dictated by his promotions to successively higher levels of command. In the initial battles of the war, Grant functioned precisely as Wellington had done: directing the course of the battle from the back of a horse. He could rally disheartened soldiers and their commanders, take charge while men were dying all around him. But as the forces he commanded grew, to finally include all the armies the Union had in the field, Grant's leadership style changed. He was able to will himself into a necessary passivity, endure long, frustrating waits while his subordinate generals, separated from him by hundreds of miles, struggled to carry out the missions he had given them. Grant was uniquely able to make the transition from battlefield commander to commander in chief, a step that requires a whole new set of skills, and abilities that do not necessarily connect with what is required at lower levels.

Consequently, to appreciate Grant's genius, we have to go forward, to see how his frustrations with incapable commanders prefigure those experienced by senior commanders in other armies in other wars. Most people know that Dwight D. Eisenhower was the supreme commander of all allied forces in Europe after fall 1943. What they may not know was that Eisenhower, like Grant, also faced personality problems and problematic generals whose abilities on the battlefield were often obscured by their behavior off the field.

The problems Eisenhower and Grant faced were by no means limited to America. The senior French generals in the First World War were also saddled with generals who had difficult personalities or were inefficient but who were almost impossible to replace due to their political connections.

Many of the problems Grant faced were problems that other generals in other countries at other times also faced. The particulars of each situation need not concern us; the point is that Grant can easily stand comparison with any of the great captains, and that his experiences in the Civil War were very much like the experiences that other great generals have encountered.

Grant managed all these problems brilliantly, but they were primarily administrative rather than purely military matters, so it is in the first part of the war that Grant's military genius can best be seen. Consequently, this study places more emphasis on the first main period of his generalship (1861–1862) than is usually the case.

+>==<+

The leadership on both sides in this war was of a very high order indeed, one reason why names like Sherman, Sheridan, Grant, Lee, and Stonewall Jackson are so familiar to Americans. We live in an age in which it is quite fashionable to debunk greatness, to turn great captains into figureheads or accidents. In some cases the process may be justified. But the leading generals of the Civil War were all men of great talent.

In fact, one of the reasons for ranking Grant so highly is that he overcame such a formidable group of adversaries. Great captains require great adversaries and it was the tragedy of the Civil War that these rivalries between great men existed. As we will see, it is exactly this tragedy that made the Civil War an incredibly sophisticated struggle, a harbinger of what was to come in the next century.

CHAPTER 1

An Ordinary Life

GRANT'S EARLY LIFE PRESENTS US WITH A VEXING PROBLEM. We know little about it, and Grant said even less. This statement is as true about biographical details as it is about his retrospective remarks on warfare. In his memoirs, considered one of the great works of American literature, Grant wrote wonderfully evocative descriptions of what he saw. He said next to nothing about what he felt, and surprisingly little about what he did, confining himself to bare descriptions of events.

Aside from being a military genius of the first order, Grant was a perfectly ordinary human being, and there is hardly anything in his childhood and youth, his family background and education, to suggest future greatness. Grant was almost forty years old when the Civil War broke out, and one scours the records of those first four decades in vain for any clues as to his greatness.

Biographers are storytellers. Very much aware that there is not much of story to tell about Grant's early years, his biographers have created one. "Triumph over Adversity" is how one of the most accomplished Grant biographers puts it, referring to a story with which almost every American is familiar: Grant, a failure in civilian life, a man with a serious drinking problem, became a great general.[1]

Although the temptation to create an interesting tale is understandable, the title of this chapter is closer to the mark. Grant's was an ordinary life. There are only a few hints to his future greatness, and those are subtle.

+>——+——<+

Ulysses S. Grant was born Hiram Ulysses Grant on April 27, 1822. His birthplace, Point Pleasant, Ohio, was a small town on the north bank of the Ohio River, about twenty-five miles to the south of Cincinnati. Through an error, his appointment to West Point was in the name of Ulysses Simpson Grant, probably owing to the fact that his mother's maiden name was Simpson. Bureaucracies being what they are, Grant was stuck with the name, and early in the war he was called "Unconditional Surrender" Grant. However, the nickname is misleading: Grant generally extended terms to his vanquished opponents that were quite generous, which, in the first years of the war, led to criticism from armchair generals in Washington.

Grant's father was a self-made man who did well in life, well enough for Ulysses to be able to work in the family business in the years directly before the war. He clearly wanted his son to excel, but the characteristics for which Grant became well known later in his life—modesty, reserve, and tolerance—are directly attributable to his mother. He took after his mother physically as well: he was slight, never weighing much more than 130 pounds, and of medium height, although his slouch often made him appear shorter than his perfectly average five foot six inches. His physical endurance is what we would expect of a son whose mother survived six childbirths in the 1820s.

Although by legend his grandfather had been a captain in the American Revolution, this is uncertain; in any event, there was no particular military strain in either side of the family.

Grant went to West Point at seventeen because it offered an excellent college education for free. The fact that Grant could pass the entrance exam suggests education and intelligence, as about half of the applicants failed it. Other than this success, and evidence that he was en expert horseman, the only sign in his early life that suggests unusual intelligence was that he managed to teach himself algebra, which, as any ordinary person who has ever tried it can attest, is an impressive feat.

But there is nothing in Grant's early years to suggest his future fame. Nor was the choice of West Point an indicator of any interest in matters military. The majority of its graduates had no real interest in a military career, but used the excellent technical education as a stepping stone in civilian life.

West Point offered one of the best modern university degrees in the world. The curriculum consciously opposed the traditional college study of Latin, rhetoric, and the classics with three major subjects: mathematics, physics, and engineering.

The only surprising point about the course of study required of all cadets was that drawing was also a subject, but there was a practical military reason for this. In the 1840s—and for decades afterwards—there were no contour maps. The West Point degree was basically a civil engineering degree, and officers were taught to size up the ground over which they would maneuver. Landscape painting and drawing was a good way of teaching this on a practical level.

The required language was French, a choice that reflected the reputation and influence of Napoleon in the study of war. As hardly any of the major works on or by Napoleon had been translated into English at this time, the clear idea was that future officers would learn enough French to enable them to read those works in the original. The dominant theorist of Grant's time was a Swiss officer, Henri Antoine Jomini, who had served under Napoleon and then written extensively about his campaigns. As Jomini's most influential work, *On the Art of War,* was not translated until 1862, the only direct exposure possible for Grant and his colleagues was by reading it in the original French. As potential military attachés to American embassies, French would also be useful, since it was the common tongue of diplomacy and statecraft.

The primacy of French theorists in Grant's time may be surprising as we are accustomed to associating science in general and military science in particular with the Germans. Carl von Clausewitz, the great German military theorist, had also fought in the Napoleonic wars, and his most famous work, *On War,* had appeared in 1832, four years before Jomini's treatise *On the Art of War.* But it languished in almost total obscurity until after Germany defeated France in 1870; the first translation did not appear until 1872.

We are told that Grant had a difficult time with French. However, given how French was taught at the time, that does not necessarily mean that he was unable to read Jomini. For that matter, we do not know precisely what portions of Jomini (and other, lesser, French military historians) were taught in class. All the early West Point records were destroyed in a fire in 1938. Thus an important part of his military formation is simply missing.

⊹⊱◆⊰⊹

Historically, the prevailing idea among Civil War historians and biographers has been that Grant was either ignorant or indifferent to military theory. The evaluation is based mostly on inferences about his language skills. This rush to judgment is understandable, and brings us to grips with one of the major difficulties in understanding Grant.

Grant was extremely reserved in discussing himself either intellectually or personally. He was an intensely private and personal individual, and, as one of his best biographers remarks, "*Taciturn* and *imperturbable* are among the most common adjectives in the lexicon of Grant commentary."[2]

His contemporaries found him puzzling, and successive biographers have found his character almost impervious to analysis. The equestrian statue of Grant on a plinth, surveying the Vicksburg battlefield, his face obscured by shadow in any light, is the perfect symbol of how little we know about the man (see photo insert). Most of it comes down to conjecture and inference.

In terms of the academic accomplishments usually seen as an indicator of intellectual ability, all we really know that is concrete can be summed up in a sentence. He entered West Point in 1839, and graduated in 1843, twenty-first in a class of thirty-nine. But it is difficult to make anything of this. There were 79 cadets in the entering class, so 40 of them failed to graduate. Depending on how we calculate these matters, Grant was either in the top quarter of his class or well towards the bottom.

Complicating matters further is a peculiarity of the West Point system. Rank was first computed according to grades, but that standing was then adjusted according to how well one met the traditional obsessions of any peacetime army with dress, deportment, and an attention to minutiae. Judging by his future indifference to such details, Grant had no interest in these matters, and since he hardly planned to make the army a career, he was justified in seeing them simply as irritations.

In a nutshell, then, based on the facts, Grant's basic character seems obscure right from the start. What little we know is derived from scattered anecdotes related by his classmates at West Point. The relevance and authenticity of these are unfortunately compromised by the fact that they all emerged long after the fact. By the time anyone had any interest in hearing about Grant's life as a cadet, he was already a very famous American.

For what it is worth, the tenor of these retrospective reminiscences is that he was reserved but well liked, said little but was listened to with respect. Given later events, these recollections may well be true, but amiability is not a very good predictor of military success, or of intellectual abilities.

For that matter, high performance in school is not a particularly accurate indicator of intelligence nor is it a very good predictor of future success. Schools and peacetime armies tend to reward people for achievements that have very little to do with success later on in life. Bernard Montgomery emerged in the Second World War as his country's most successful commander, one of military history's great captains. In later years, as a field marshal, he was called on to be present at the graduation ceremonies for Sandhurst, the British equivalent of West Point. When Great Britain's most distinguished students were called out to be honored at their graduation ceremony, Montgomery was heard to remark that they would: "never be heard of again."[3] The comment seems harsh, but in reality it is charitable. When the Civil War began, many of Grant's more distinguished West Point colleagues failed to live up to the promise of their early careers.

Given Grant's achievements as a general, and the fact that he was twice elected to the presidency, we would assume that anyone who predicted his future success, based on his personal knowledge of the young man, would have stepped up and told the world about his judgment. The absence of such testimony is suggestive. What exists are extremely divided evaluations of the man, evaluations that began during his lifetime and have never ceased.

Because Grant did not show any outward signs of greatness or leadership, or evince any particular interest in or aptitude for the military until he was forty years old, it is easy to see why his character befuddled his contemporaries and his chroniclers. Most of us find the model exemplified by Napoleon or Alexander the Great more congenial, to cite only the most famous examples. Here were men whose achievements began at an early age. Napoleon, born in 1769, was already a French general winning stunning victories while still in his twenties. Alexander the Great had already conquered an enormous part of the known world by the time of his death at age thirty-three.

In the broader context of military history, of course, it is equally possible to find another path, men who emerged as great captains only later in life: Julius Caesar and Marlborough, who, although less familiar to Americans, is generally regarded by British military historians as his country's greatest general. This path would be Grant's. Marlborough never fought "a battle he did not win, nor besieged a town he did not take," in the words of one eighteenth century biographer.[4] The same could be said of Grant. Both men became generals relatively late in life, and proved themselves masters of the battlefield.

There are always analysts who will seek the key to such success in other factors, stripping the great general of responsibility for his achievements, but Grant was the sole architect of his victories. These achievements suggest a talent bordering on genius. The question for the biographer is to what extent can we divine that genius in the young man.

⊰⊱

Genius is different from success. The question to ask is not can we see indicators of future success in his early life; it is, can we see signs of genius there? Or, for those uncomfortable with the word and its implications, can we see signs of the sort of unusually high aptitude that are often missed? Put that way, Grant's character becomes much less of a puzzle. It is fairly easy to detect three important signs indicating that Grant was an unusual young man.

The first is an extraordinary capacity for abstract thought, as evidenced by his ability in mathematics. It is, interestingly enough, a trait that Grant shared with Napoleon, whose mathematical talents shone out amidst otherwise middling scholastic achievements.

As we shall see, one of Grant's characteristics as a general was his ability to compute precisely all the quantitative data required to make correct decisions on the battlefield. Again, although one might suppose that this skill is less required in the computing age, it is even more important, given the enormous amounts of information available to decision makers.

We have two very concrete indicators of this capacity. On the one hand, Grant taught himself algebra. This is no minor feat. On the other hand, we have one of the very few—almost the only—revealing personal remarks Grant ever made about what he wanted to do, that he hoped to return to West Point and teach mathematics. Mastery of mathematics is one thing: seeing it as a career is quite another.

The second key to understanding Grant's genius is his talent in drawing and painting. As we remarked earlier, the subject was taught at West Point for practical reasons. The German officer training schools that were being created at this time taught this principle religiously. Mastery of the terrain of the battlefield was indispensable. As Field Marshal Montgomery lectured British officers over and over again during the Second World War, it was one of the main reasons why the Germans were such formidable opponents.

It might be supposed that in an era of satellite photography and digital images being transmitted in real time, this skill would no longer be required. On the contrary; the highly mobile world of modern combat is three-dimensional, so the skill of visualization is even more of a necessity now than it was in Grant's time.

At West Point, future officers were in theory trained not only to read maps, but to produce their own sketches based on what they saw. The key word here is theory. More than one Civil War general was unable to understand the basic principle of the contour map. Grant, on the contrary, seems to have had an almost instinctive grasp of the terrain. He had a remarkable faculty for casting his eye over the ground and then retaining a picture of it in his mind.

Drawing, which requires an understanding of perspective, is one aid to learning how to visualize terrain. Consequently, all students at West Point took lessons in the subject. Where Grant was an exception was in the quality of his work. Unlike many amateurs, Grant's landscapes reveal a sure sense of perspective as well as an almost photographic reproduction of the scene.

Both Hitler and Churchill were artists as well. Contrary to popular legend, Hitler was a decent enough painter to be able to sell his paintings of Viennese scenes to tourists. Hitler and Churchill preferred to paint landscapes; what sets Grant apart, as best we can judge from the surviving works, is his interest in portraits, often of unlikely subjects, such as horses and Indians. Curiously, when Grant drew a horse, he did not draw a military charger, he drew a horse peacefully standing in a pasture. When he drew Indians, he drew them engaged in ordinary life, as though he saw them as ordinary people—an intriguing insight, given the attitudes towards Indians prevalent in American society at the time.[5]

The combination of interests in two wildly different areas, algebra and painting, suggests a character with an unusual combination of skills and interests, and this is reinforced by one of the few things we know about Grant's intellectual behavior and the third sign of his exceptional nature. He read voraciously. Curiously his preferred readings were novels, not military histories, although in later years he frequently amazed witnesses by his detailed and extensive knowledge of the subject. Clearly he had read widely in the field. But this was a given for aspiring officers; the curiosity is the interest in fiction, particularly for Anglo-Americans, who have historically seen the idea of the novel as entirely separate from the notion of history.

But this is a false dichotomy. Globally speaking, army officers have often seen certain kinds of novels as being extremely relevant to their profession. For a generation of French and German officers, for example, Tolstoy's *War and Peace* was a far better portrait of what warfare was like than any military history. Much the same thing could be said of American officers and Anton Myrer's *Once an Eagle* (1968).

The reasoning is not hard to see: novels can provide great insights into character, shape lessons about behavior that give us a greater understanding of humanity. Just as abstract thought is necessary for the great commander, so is an understanding of the men he must send to their deaths, as well as the chaos of the battlefield. Again and again witnesses to Grant's generalship comment on his understanding of the officers and men who served in his command, and in the history of his major campaigns that follows we will see examples of this.

Although usually unremarked upon, there are two aspects of Grant's novel reading that should be pointed out. In comparison with other educated people, those who read literature tend to be able to read very quickly, and to keep complicated events in their minds. Grant's voracious reading indicates a mental quickness. In the nineteenth century, novelists were masters of the language, and this was particularly the case with Sir Walter Scott, one of Grant's favorites. This immersion, when coupled with his mathematical abilities, probably explains why Grant, despite his modest rural education, was able to write so clearly and effectively, so that his memoirs stand out as a model of good writing.

The unusually broad background, when coupled with his abilities at abstract thought, go far to explain his perceived lack of interest in the narrowly focused military theories that so gripped many of his contemporaries at West Point. Like Napoleon and Wellington, he was not so much contemptuous of armchair retrospectives in which basic principles of warfare were allegedly deduced, he was simply indifferent to them. Or, to put it another way, the fashionable military ideas of many American officers about warfare looked backwards to what had been laboriously distilled from Napoleon. Grant's view of warfare looked forward to the world of the great Prussian commanders of the 1860s, for whom strategy was not some arcane discipline but simply common sense.

To be blunt about it: during the war, Grant took risks and proved to have an intuition that many of his commanders did not quite understand. His apparent reticence then, although perhaps originating in shyness and a genuine reserve, was most likely the silence of a man who realizes there is little point in talking to people who are not ready to hear what he has to say.

When taken all together, this unusual combination of interests and intellectual achievements suggests a mind of a very high order. It also explains his perceived reticence and his relative indifference to minutiae. He was, in a word, bored, because nothing that was required of him presented any sort of challenge. In the tightly controlled world of early nineteenth-century America, there was little opportunity for one of the classical signs of genius, asocial behavior, and this was certainly true in Grant's case, given his parents. Quietness, amiability, and a certain indifference to achievements, are also good indicators of genius, so it is no surprise to find them in Grant.

Nor is the next step in his life unusual.

In order to pay for his education, Grant had to serve in the army. Given his horsemanship, and his love of horses, he had wanted to be in the cavalry, but was assigned instead to an infantry regiment based in Saint Louis, Missouri.

To understand this next phase of Grant's life, it is necessary to consider two characteristics of peacetime army life. The first is virtually unique to America. In 1843 the United States Army was essentially a national police force, and organized as such, with small packets of soldiers scattered all over the country. In peacetime, junior officers had very little to do. Of course in those days, this was true of officers everywhere. They had relatively few men to supervise, actual maneuvers and what we might call training occupied a surprisingly small percentage of their day. As the European aphorism put it: they were expected to die for their country, but might live as they pleased in the meantime.

Their main enemy was boredom, which led to gambling, drunkenness, and scandals involving the wives and daughters of the towns where they were stationed. If there was less of this in the American army, it was largely because of how the garrisons were distributed, and the dominance of Puritanism in American public life.

Thus, like a good many young men then and now, Grant developed an interest in women. And like any upright young man, his interest was romantic, his goal marriage. Grant fell in love with the sister of one of his fellow officers, and began courting her. Julia Dent was an attractive young woman whose father was a somewhat conceited man with pretensions to an aristocratic position as a Southern landowner that he did not in fact possess. What he did possess were slaves. Despite the close affiliation of Grant's parents, and particularly his mother, with the American Methodists, for whom slavery was anathema, Grant was deeply in love.

There's nothing unusual about young men pursuing the object of their heart's desire over the objections of both sets of parents. What is unusual in Grant's case is that he not only persuaded Julia to marry him, but they proved a remarkably stable couple, despite the various changes of fortune that they would experience over the next decades. Of all the great captains of history, Grant is the most uxorious. Whatever his weaknesses were—and in years to come much would be made of them—a wandering eye was not one of them. What is evident is that, even as a young man, the sum of Grant's contradictions and interests and convictions reveal a remarkable individual, clearly standing out from the crowd.

Freshly minted lieutenants serving out their time were not the most attractive of matches for a young woman in the 1840s: the pay was poor, living conditions bad, and their life expectancy—should there be any fighting—very short. Whether or not Julia would have married Ulysses had there not been a war in the offing is an open question. But a war with Mexico was brewing, and the normalcy of the peacetime military was about to change.

CHAPTER 2

From Mexico to Galena

On April 25, 1846 the United States declared war on Mexico.
Decades later, Grant would reflect on the folly of the Mexican ad-
venture, which he linked explicitly to the tragedy of the Civil War: "The
Southern Rebellion was largely the outgrowth of the Mexican war. We
got our punishment in the most sanguinary and expensive war of modern times," Grant observed in his memoirs.[1] Whether or not this represented his thinking in 1845 is another matter entirely; in any event the
thought has now become virtually a historical cliché. Everyone knew
that the annexation of Texas would precipitate a conflict with Mexico;
the usual explanation for this is that the annexation was greatly desired
because it would augment the number of states where slavery was still
practiced.

But the observation says a good deal about Grant, who simply did not talk about warfare in military terms. One of his few comments about the peacetime army he found himself in speaks volumes both as to his point of view and his acumen:

> Too many of the older officers, when they came to command posts, made it a study to think what orders they could publish to annoy their subordinates. . . . I noticed, however, a few years later, when the Mexican war broke out, that most of this class of officers discovered they were possessed of disabilities which entirely incapacitated them from active field service. They were right; but they did not always give their disease the right name. (*Memoirs*, 18)

Unfortunately, Grant's summary of his experiences in the war is blandly unspecific. One looks in vain for comments about tactics or strategy. Instead, Grant's emphasis was generally on the psychological makeup of men going into battle. As and as his own initial baptism of fire approached, he was candid in his admission that "I felt sorry I had enlisted" (43).

But Grant proved himself a steady and resourceful officer. He was promptly made the quartermaster of the Fourth Infantry Regiment, a position of great responsibility for a lieutenant of twenty-four, as the quartermaster was tasked with seeing that the troops in the regiment were supplied with food, ammunition, and everything else they required to fight effectively. Despite his candid honesty about his feelings the first time he was under fire, Grant protested his promotion: he wanted to continue as a combat commander.

Grant managed both to serve as quartermaster and see combat. During the fight for Monterrey (September 21–23, 1846), the regiment was pinned down by Mexican sharpshooters while awaiting reinforcements. Because of the intensity of the fighting, they were running out of ammunition. Grant mounted a horse and rode off through the proverbial hail of bullets to get more ammunition for the regiment. He survived only because of his prowess as a horseman; he hung on to the saddle horn and one stirrup, keeping the horse between himself and the enemy.

Although the war with Mexico is little remembered today, American casualties (the number of injured, killed, captured or missing in a military engagement), expressed as a percentage of men deployed, were the highest in American history. The numbers were slightly higher even than in the Civil War, and quite commensurate with the losses sustained in the savage wars of Frederick the Great, Marlborough, and Napoleon.[2] Given the high casualty rate, Grant's survival unscathed, despite having been in combat, was an achievement.

Grant fought all the way through the bloody struggle in Mexico. He was therefore inoculated against the horror of battle. Inoculated, but not indifferent or callous. In fact, the only other historical anecdote we have of Grant in Mexico (aside from his wild ride for ammunition) is of his caring for American soldiers wounded during the Battle of Monterrey. He was always deeply moved by wounded soldiers, and invariably concerned about their treatment. But he understood now in practice what before he had only understood intellectually: the ordeal of combat, the ordeal of seeing one's friends killed.

If Grant appeared unmoved by the slaughter in later battles, it was because he had already gone through that intensely personal experience when he was a young man. The Civil War did not require Grant to prove his personal courage, either to himself or others, which probably accounts for his remarkable calm and steadiness during battle.

Grant's experiences as quartermaster are rightly cited as invaluable to his development as a soldier. Wellington learned the importance of logistics during his campaigns in India; Mexico was Grant's India. It is instructive to find that on assuming direct command during a battle, one of Grant's first acts was always to ensure that his soldiers had ample supplies of ammunition. Clearly this concern can be traced back to September 1846 when the youthful lieutenant had to run the gauntlet of enemy fire to secure this valuable commodity.

A good deal of his success in the first part of the Civil War was a function of his understanding of logistics. The emphasis Grant placed on logistics would become a trait of American military operations in the future, as American soldiers had to fight all over the world. In each case they were expected to fight and win battles because of their logistical superiority, which can be considered part of Grant's legacy.

There is of course another rather obvious point to be made about the relevance of Grant's experiences in Mexico. The two American armies that invaded the country advanced through bleak and hostile territory. Grant served under Zachary Taylor, whose men crossed the Rio Grande and marched all the way to Mexico City—an advance of hundreds of miles. General Winfield Scott landed an expeditionary force at Vera Cruz and, following in the footsteps of the great Spanish *conquistadore,* Cortez, led his men to the same destination.

Wellington is reported to have said that Scott's expedition was one of the most incredible feats in military history. It was. Grant had the remarkable examples of both Taylor and Scott laid before him, examples of what could be accomplished by a general bold enough to take risks, and prudent enough to enable them to succeed. Grant would replicate these daring offensive moves during the Civil War.

It is tempting to see in these experiences in Mexico the germs of Grant's great thrust into Mississippi in 1863, and his ordering of Sherman to make his even greater thrust through Georgia to the coast in 1864. But to view Grant's boldness only in this way is insufficient, since the Confederate officers Grant would oppose had also fought in Mexico, as had more than a few of the Union officers. The experiences of the Mexican War were common to most of the senior commanders, and Grant was hardly the only one to reflect on the lessons of that bitter struggle.

It is this that gives the Civil War a character that is unique among major wars: the commanders on both sides knew each other, sometimes only by reputation, but often surprisingly well. James Longstreet, who eventually became one of Robert E. Lee's most talented commanders, had been assigned to the Fourth Infantry a year before Grant. The young officers served together, fighting their way through Mexico, and became close friends. Longstreet even served as the best man at Grant's wedding. Great commanders often try to learn all they can about their opponents, but they learn from afar and their information is filtered through others. In the Civil War the knowledge was often personal and direct.

Grant was not the only officer who used his knowledge of his former officers in divining what they would do now that they were his enemies. But he had studied his peers closely. Close enough so that he seems to have had absolute confidence in how some of them would react when he confronted them on the battlefield. That knowledge goes a long way towards explaining his confidence that he would be successful in fighting them.

While Grant was in Mexico, he learned much by observing the tactics of Zachary Taylor. Grant was just a lowly lieutenant, but the American force Taylor commanded was very small so Grant could watch him closely. There were only about 75,000 men serving in the whole Mexican War, and neither Scott nor Taylor ever had many more than 10,000 men under their command for any one engagement. Indeed, Scott's expeditionary force was hardly the size of an infantry division. This gave Grant the unusual opportunity of observing the commander of the army in action, and it is pretty clear that he was deeply impressed by Zachary Taylor's leadership style.

Taylor was a first rate general whose disheveled appearance was a complete repudiation of what Grant had seen emphasized both at West Point and in the peacetime army. Also, contemporary descriptions of Taylor usually imply that he had bad posture. Given Grant's unmilitary bearing and his rumpled clothing later in life, it is logical to conclude that Grant was simply following Taylor's lead, and most historians have jumped to that conclusion. But Taylor was hardly the only great general who eschewed fancy uniforms with lots of gold braid. Frederick the Great went about in patched and tattered cloaks; Wellington, in the Spanish campaigns, dressed like he was going on hunt, and one of his best generals carried an umbrella instead of a sword. Grant may very well have taken a certain pleasure in following their example and deliberately countering the sort of military finery exemplified by French and Austrian officers and sedulously imitated by their counterparts in North and South America.

A more casual attire was more than a sartorial affectation, however. As the range and lethality of the standard infantry weapon increased, generals became much more vulnerable on the battlefield. One sensible approach was to dress in a way that did not instantly call out one's rank. Dressing down for the battlefield and the campaign was common sense. It was part and parcel of the same logic that would soon dictate that a common uniform be worn by all the soldiers in any one army. There had been far too many Napoleonic friendly fire incidents caused by confusion about uniforms—and in the first serious battle of the Civil War, Big Bethel, Union troops started blasting away at other Union troops who had gone into battle wearing uniforms the same color as those worn by many Confederate soldiers.

+≻═══≺+

Grant picked up more than how to dress from Zachary Taylor, though. He was impressed by Taylor's equanimity—a virtue rather difficult to adhere to in the heat of battle, particularly when you are the person responsible for seeing to it that the battle is won. During one of the first major battles in Mexico, when a somewhat panicky subordinate turned to Taylor and said that the battle was lost, Taylor is alleged to have pointed to his infantry and remarked, "But they don't know it."

Whether this actually happened or not, this anecdote could also perfectly describe Grant under fire. He had confidence in his men, and returned that confidence back to them by his equanimity on the battlefield.

What impressed Grant the most, however, was the realization of the heavy responsibility that Taylor bore as the commander of the American forces. We speak of the burden of command, and it is no light burden. Grant was fortunate to be able to see how that burden was borne, to begin to apprehend what it must be like, and he was intelligent enough, perceptive enough, to grasp its character.

Experience, the fact of being there, does not count for everything. Napoleon once remarked that by this standard, his horse would have been a great general. But when experience is linked with perception, it counts for a great deal. And this explains why Grant so easily assumed his commands in 1861, and why he can not be said to have had a traditional learning curve.

In Mexico, Grant saw warfare in all its horror and complexity unfold, absorbed what he saw, and then spent years thinking about it. Similarly, even though he was years younger than Grant when he became a general, Napoleon's first moves on assuming command were also virtually flawless: like Athena springing from the forehead of Zeus, a fully grown adult.

+>====<+

The problem with studying great generals is that often their military genius is only manifested when they become generals and fight wars. Although it is logical to see Grant's experiences in the Mexican War as preparing him for future command, the armies on both sides in the Civil War were full of generals who had also fought in Mexico as junior officers. Most of them did poorly as generals. So it is just as logical to infer that Grant, like Napoleon and Wellington, already possessed the secrets of great leadership on the battlefield and his Mexican experiences simply added to his arsenal.

It is in Mexico that for the first time we have a concrete indicator from someone else of Grant's abilities. Grant's appointment to West Point had come from Thomas Hamer, an Ohio congressman. Hamer volunteered to serve as an officer during the Mexican War, and caught up with Grant in Mexico. Hamer knew Grant's father, but not Grant himself. But as Hamer got to know the young lieutenant during the tedious hours of the campaign, he prophesied a brilliant career ahead for Grant as an officer. Hamer's evaluation is important, as it does not represent a retrospective judgment penned long after Grant's successes. Nor did he have a chance to go back and revise it, as he fell ill during the campaign and died before the end of the war.

Unfortunately for Grant's immediate military prospects, the war with Mexico only lasted sixteen months. With the fighting over, the army promptly reverted to its peacetime obsessions with being a territorial police force. Combat performance counted for next to nothing as the troops were distributed to isolated outposts all over the country, where most of them had little to do except get in trouble.

In Grant's case, the problem was compounded by what in most armies would have been regarded as a monumental act of folly. In 1848, the young lieutenant, who had fallen in love back in Missouri in 1843, finally persuaded the young woman, Julia Dent, to marry him.

The problem for the Grants was sadly typical. It was basically impossible for them to live on his pay, and the army bases to which he was assigned were desolate outposts in the extremes of the country, particularly in the Pacific Northwest. Young Julia, who quickly became pregnant, was no more suited for this life than her husband. That meant a separation, and that in turn led to depression and the bottle for Grant, something exacerbated by the grim determination of the Army to revert as quickly as possible to its peacetime routines.

By 1854, a miserable Grant resigned his commission and went into the civilian life he had always planned to resume after he had fulfilled his military obligation. All sorts of wild stories began to circulate as to why he had resigned from the Army, none of them flattering, and the rumors would come back with a vengeance once the war broke out.

However, there is no real evidence to support any of these stories other than the bare bones of being ridden mercilessly by his superior officer. Army officers resigned in unusually large numbers that year, and the most probable cause for Grant's decision is his frustration with peacetime military life and his desire to be with his wife.[3]

It is from this period that Grant's reputation as a drunk would emerge, and through embellishment and repetition, the legend of Grant the alcoholic became firmly lodged in the public consciousness.[4] Amplified considerably by the usual smears that any successful person accumulates, this rumor would dog him forever. Surprisingly, the extent of Grant's drinking and the degree to which he may be fairly said to have been an alcoholic, is difficult to determine, particularly given the relatively few first-person accounts we have regarding actual episodes of drunkenness.

There is no doubt that Grant drank, and that in his late twenties and early thirties as a young officer, he drank too much. Medically speaking, that does not make him an alcoholic.[5] If we restrict ourselves to witnesses speaking on the basis of direct experience, Grant may have been an episodic alcohol abuser in the early 1850s, but he seems to have overcome the problem long before the Civil War began. There were probably regressive incidents during the war, but the occurrences were too sporadic to warrant even a diagnosis of episodic abuse. There is no evidence he was ever impaired during the war, unable to carry out his duties; no evidence that his personal relationships were impaired; and no real instances of him putting himself in harm's way.

Although rumors of his drinking were brought up again and again during the war, Grant's promotions occurred rapidly. A civilian in April 1861 with his military experience seven years behind him, he was appointed a colonel and given command of a regiment in May 1861, and was made a brigadier general later that month. Less than a year later, March 1862, he was promoted to Major General. In February 1864, Grant was promoted again, and put in charge of all the Union armies, becoming only the second man in American history to be promoted to lieutenant general.

Although it is widely assumed that alcohol abuse either worsens or recurs steadily for any given individual, about one in every five cases is able to "achieve long-term abstinence without any type of active treatment."[6] That seems to have been the case with Grant. Definitions of alcoholism, however, are also culturally determined, and in the United States in the 1850s the definitions were written in stone. In Grant's day the drunkard was seen as a moral degenerate, one given to vice, and undifferentiated vice at that. The epithet of drunkard was probably the worst epithet that could be hurled at a man, as it implied every sort of depravity and vice, every sort of moral weakness imaginable.

That this was a judgment peculiar to nineteenth-century America hardly needs to be pointed out. In a European army—as in most European countries—no one would have thought much about Grant's drinking, however it may have been defined. It was assumed that young officers would have vices, and the two that were the most troublesome were gambling and fights, since the former could lead to bribes and the latter to getting killed. Misadventures with alcohol and women were more or less assumed and tolerated.

The attitude towards alcoholism in America also explains why Grant's perfectly normal life from 1854 to 1861 is often characterized as a complete failure, as he engaged in a bitter struggle to support himself and his family. Given his "problem," he had to fail, and many accounts of Grant's life underline the failures behind his every success. The idea that soldiers are failures in civilian life has a perennial appeal to Americans, one no less deeply seated for being completely untrue, at least in Grant's case.

The reality was rather prosaic. Grant struggled to make a living for his growing family, tried his hand at farming, and finally moved back to Galena, Illinois to work in the family business. He was hard-working, a devoted family man, and while he was not much of a success in civilian life, he was not a failure either and his life was ordinary to the point of banality. Retrospective accounts of the magnitude of his failure during the period from 1854 to 1861 should therefore be taken with a grain of salt. By 1859, the Grants were comfortable enough.

The family's home in Galena was a well-built brick house and nicely situated—a far more substantial dwelling than the vast majority of Americans enjoyed at the time.[7] Moreover, Grant had something that satisfied him, something for which many men would willingly sacrifice a great deal: a devoted wife and a family.

<hr />

In those years, Grant also managed to earn the respect of at least one man who was destined to play an important role both in his life and in the history of the United States. Elihu B. Washburne, born in Maine, had become a resident of Galena, Illinois, and was elected to congress. Washburne was a shrewd politician whose advice and good counsel helped shape Lincoln's response to the great crisis of Secession that was gripping the country in the years before the outbreak of the Civil War. He was an educated man with a broad view of the world, as he had studied law at Harvard and been one of the editors of Maine's *Kennebec Journal.*

Washburne knew Grant, and would push his military career toward advancement at every opportunity. As a Republican congressman from the same state as Lincoln, and his enthusiastic supporter, Washburne was ideally situated to have the president's attention. Once the war began, his friendship with Grant would be crucial to the general's career.

However, when he first moved to Galena, Grant had no thoughts of returning to the army. By all accounts, he was a happy man, and the Grants a happy couple. They remained so until the end of their lives, sleeping in the same bed whenever they were together.

But their domestic tranquility was about to be shattered. On April 16, 1861, the Civil War broke out. A year later, Grant was a famous (even notorious) and controversial figure. Two years later, he was hailed as the savior of the Union. By the end of the war he was seen as the greatest general the country had ever produced.

CHAPTER 3

Tactics and Technology
in the Age of Grant

THE UNION AND CONFEDERATE GENERALS whose ranks Grant would join in May 1861 faced new and unprecedented changes in the nature of warfare. Developments in the basic technology of firearms forced a substantial revision of methods of army deployment and fighting from those of the previous two hundred years. A brief consideration of those changes is necessary in order to understand the remarkable nature of Grant's achievements.

The basics of military deployment and maneuver, brilliantly codified by Frederick the Great in the 1750s, were all predicated on smoothbore muskets and cannon. However complex the actual maneuvers were, as generals jockeyed for an advantage on the field of battle, they were all based on a simple calculation. The smoothbore musket operated like a child's pea shooter. The bullet rattled around inside the gun tube, resulting in a weapon that was wildly inaccurate. Forty or fifty yards was the maximum killing zone, and although the wobbly trajectory of the irregular mass fired resulted in a highly lethal projectile, accuracy was so poor that even if your opponent was thirty or forty yards away, you had a very good chance of missing him entirely. Although armies liked to pretend otherwise, the accuracy of sustained volleys of smoothbore muskets was unbelievably bad. In an average battle of the Napoleonic wars, 3.5 million bullets were fired and there were only 8,000 men killed in action.[1]

These factors were basically a constant. A volley delivered at sixty yards would kill very few men, and the bulk of the attacking infantry would then be able to reach their enemy while he was reloading, as muzzle-loading muskets took time to reload. In theory, well-trained soldiers could fire and reload three times in a minute, but the judgment of most eighteenth-century gunnery experts was that in the heat of battle soldiers were lucky to fire and reload more than once per minute. At such close ranges, the charging infantry would catch their opponents trying to reload. Seeing this, the soldiers reloading their muskets would break ranks and run away.

This meant that generals could stand well out of range and direct the battle in person from distances of less than two hundred yards, surveying the scene without field glasses. Cavalry units, deployed a few hundred yards back, could wait patiently out of range. A galloping horse could cover the distance even more quickly than charging infantry, closing those two hundred yards in less than three minutes. As a result, cavalry charges were extremely effective over short distances. Once the infantry turned to flee, the horsemen could easily run them down.

Histories of all the armed battles during this period, including the Civil War, are packed with accounts of hand-to-hand combats and bayonet charges, but once medical services began counting casualties by type, it was found that few men were actually speared or sabered. Union medical records catalogue only 56 deaths from edged weapons, leading its authors to the conclusion that "it is apparent that as used against the American troops on later wars, and as against the Northern troops in the Civil War, as judged by admission to hospital, the bayonet and saber were military weapons of little significance."[2]

Rifling (cutting grooves along the length of the inside of the barrel), which had become more common since the Revolutionary War, greatly increased the depth of the killing field. At a hundred yards, a marksman could hit a human-sized target nine times out of ten. At three hundred yards, he could hit his target half the time, and a sharpshooter would still have an accuracy of better than 90 percent.[3] As the accuracy improved, so did the rate of fire.[4] Generals trying to direct battles at close range suddenly became prime targets. Trying to close the gap, whether it was fifty yards or three hundred, whether on horse or on foot, now became suicidal. Everything had changed.

Or had it? Between the end of the Mexican War and the start of the Civil War, American, British, and European officers tried to figure out what the rifling change meant, and with widely differing results. Broadly speaking, some (these ideas crossed national boundaries) argued that the noise, confusion, and disarray of actual combat would nullify the advantages of the new weaponry. Others argued that tactics would have to change dramatically. A third group derived from the study of Napoleon the interesting conclusion that wars would no longer be won by battles, but by seizing enemy territory—cities, ports, and railroad depots. The great age of military theory had begun.

Whether Grant was aware of these arguments, however, is difficult to say. Grant spent the time before the war chopping wood and tending store. We don't know what he read or what he thought during this period any more than we know very much about what he absorbed at West Point. Like most people who live in the real world, trying to make a living as best they can, Grant was skeptical about theories.

He had a particular reason to be skeptical. As we noted earlier, a West Point degree was touted as a stepping stone to greater achievement in civilian life, precisely because the degree was technical and modern, as opposed to a degree in the classics that was the hallmark of nineteenth-century colleges. If this theory had been correct Grant would have been a wealthy man as a civilian, as very few people graduated from college in those days, particularly with a degree in engineering. But Grant was just barely getting by.

Then there was the little matter of Grant's drinking. According to another widely believed theory of the age, a man who drank like Grant did when he was in the army should have been little more than a derelict. But there he was, happily married and raising family.

Grant's experiences in the real world thus either confirmed his realism or converted him to it. Whichever was the case, the result was the same. He approached military matters with a good deal of skepticism, drawing on practical knowledge gained from his time in combat and his observations of Zachary Taylor and his fellow officers.

Grant was a realist. In the world of theory, the rifled musket made frontal attacks suicidal. But in Mexico, Grant had seen over and over that this was not necessarily the case. The point that struck him most forcibly was that European generals fought their battles on terrain that was entirely different from what would be found in the United States. American terrain was the sort that European generals avoided at all costs: rough, wooded country, cut with gulleys and streams, marked by swollen rivers with wildly varying water levels.[5] In such terrain, Grant felt, new weapons were not going to be as effective as people assumed. The clear fields of fire that theorists envisioned simply didn't exist in America. Professional officers in Europe and Great Britain were grappling with this problem as well, unable to come to conclusion one way or another, with one school of thought arguing that the new technology had changed everything, the other arguing that it had changed much less than people thought.

<hr>

Despite writing a lengthy account of his military life, the famous memoirs, Grant said next to nothing about the nuts and bolts of combat. The reason his memoirs have such an elevated reputation in American literature is precisely because he does not discuss military arcana. As a result, we mostly have to judge him from his actions, and from the very few comments he made about battle.

One of these comments, perhaps the most important, was this: "The only way to whip an army is to go out and fight it."[6] This is one of the very few craft-related comments Grant ever made, and so we have to give it a good deal of weight. This idea is a direct contradiction of one of the basic tenets of military theory of the time, that wars could be won simply by seizing territory. This idea was exemplified by the attitudes of Union generals like Henry Halleck and Don Carlos Buell, who explained to their subordinates that it was no longer necessary even to fight battles: wars could be won simply by occupying the enemy's territory step by step.

At the same time, the notion that you must "fight" to win suggests a skepticism about the impact of the new technology on the battlefield. While Grant said very little about how one should fight wars, what little he said implied volumes and was very much in the order of some of Napoleon's most famous maxims.

Nor is it difficult to see why Grant would make such a statement, which challenged the theories of his peers. The idea that you could win by seizing territory contradicted everything that he had read and seen. In June 1815, Napoleon still had Paris and all of France, but he still lost the war because his defeated soldiers simply abandoned the field at Waterloo and went home. It did no good to have a country if you lacked an army. Grant had also experienced this firsthand in Mexico: the Mexicans did not lose the war because they lost the capital; they lost the capital because they had already lost the war.

Grant, unlike Frederick the Great, Napoleon and many of Grant's contemporaries, but like Wellington, said very little about his craft. He brought his mother's reticence to his profession. And, as we shall see, the few insights into warfare he offers in his writings concentrate on psychology, not technique or technology. For that reason, historians have always been somewhat bewildered by the man, but, judging by his actions, it is not difficult to grasp the principles that Grant had derived from his study of warfare.

Grant possessed, in other words, that shrewd sense of strategy and tactics articulated by Helmuth von Moltke the Elder: the basic principles of warfare scarcely go beyond common sense.[7] His basic response to new technology was simple. Obvious adjustments were needed: the old deployment tactics, which favored soldiers moving up in columns, was as suicidal as the idea of massed ranks advancing as on parade, or using cavalry charges.

This understanding can be seen in Grant's first directives to his troops, as early as the orders given at Shiloh. Here we find an emphasis on extended lines of skirmishers, in order to ensure that the advancing troops would not be slaughtered by the long-range musketry that was made possible by rifling.

The other solution to this problem was maneuvering. Grant, like Lee, was a master of troop deployments. In Grant's case, this meant hitting the enemy with overwhelming force where he was least prepared for it, so that by the time battle was joined, the enemy had already lost. The skirmishes that led up to the fall of Vicksburg are textbook examples.

As far as it was possible, Grant preferred surprise attacks, and attacks from the flanks as a means of getting around the great increase in the killing range. Again and again we find him shifting his troops on the battlefield so as to hit the enemy from the side, Chattanooga being perhaps the most outstanding example. Flank attacks, surprise attacks, and the choice of ground could all be used to close the distance between the forces. Letting one's enemy exhaust himself by attacking first, so that one could then charge a demoralized and exhausted foe that might well be out of ammunition also worked.

So did boxing the enemy in so he had to choose between dying and quitting—provided your enemy could be certain of being decently treated. The question Grant most often asked of his subordinates as battles progressed pertained to the numbers of prisoners taken. He understood that this item of data was an important indicator of the enemy's determination to fight. Here too Grant was far ahead of his contemporaries in Washington, and his insistence on treating those who surrendered well became firmly enshrined in American military traditions, as evidenced by the massive German surrenders to American forces during the Second World War.

+>==<+

So although the rifled musket in theory made traditional warfare a supremely deadly business, giving rise to an interpretation of the Civil War as a conflict in which to attack was to die, this was really only the case when the commanders had not thought out viable alternatives. Grant only authorized frontal attacks on a few occasions, and in each case usually at the behest of his subordinate commanders.

These assaults were horrific affairs, but although the legend of the Civil War as ghastly slaughter is well entrenched, it is hardly supported by the data. On July 1, 1916, at the Battle of the Somme, the British Army suffered 60,000 casualties in a few hours, nearly 20,000 of them fatal. By contrast, combined Union and Confederate losses at Gettysburg, the bloodiest battle of the Civil War, were over the two days of fighting, roughly 8,000 dead and nearly 80,000 casualties.[8]

That armies were still working out the problems of frontal attacks half a century later suggests how difficult they were to solve, and it makes much clearer just how good Grant was at his craft. In fact, the problem was so difficult that after the First World War, it was widely assumed that advances in technology had made offensive operations futile. It was only after the successful German offensives of 1939 through 1941 that this notion changed. Military professionals began to see that successful offensive operations were possible, and that the new technologies that were being employed on the battlefield did not give the defense any particular advantage.

After 1939 and the outbreak of the Second World War, it became increasingly clear that airpower could make massive offensive operations feasible. By the Korean War, the use of massive amounts of high explosives, mostly delivered from the air, became an American signature in combat. Most recently in 2003 in Iraq, the U.S. army backed troops on the ground with simultaneous air assaults that allowed the invasion to move swiftly and smoothly.

From his experiences in the Mexican War, Grant had seen the fallacy in assuming that the defense automatically had an advantage. Artillery, properly handled, made defensive positions untenable. Moreover, by 1860, there had been a development in gunnery that paralleled what had been going on in muskets.

Traditionally, artillery consisted of muzzle-loading smoothbore cannons that fired either solid shot (cannon balls) or shrapnel, which was an anti-personnel device.[9] So cannon were basically just enormous smoothbore muskets. They were categorized by the weight of their projectiles—a 6-pounder, the standard field gun of the United States army before the war, fired a solid piece of iron that weighed six pounds.

The maximum range of a smoothbore cannon was about fifteen hundred yards, but the accuracy was horrible, so gunners liked to be much closer, typically at three or four hundred yards. At seven hundred yards, even the largest of smoothbore cannons, the 24-pounders, weren't going to do appreciable damage to a masonry and earth fort.

With the development of rifled cannon, however, everything changed. Had the Civil War been fought two decades earlier, the forts that protected all the ports of the Confederacy—which could easily be constructed in other places—would have given it an almost insurmountable advantage. But Grant, watching the latest developments in artillery, realized that innovations of gun design made defensive fortifications nothing more than earthenware tombs.

The technology was quite new. The American engineer Robert Parrott's first weapon, a 10-pounder, was only patented in 1860.[10] So the Civil War was the first major struggle in which the new guns were deployed; officers on both sides found themselves having to deal with an entirely new situation in which fortifications no longer offered their historical advantages. They neither guaranteed the ability of the defender to hold strategically important positions nor offered his men the security of protection against hostile fire.

Although both sides relied extensively on rifled cannon, Grant was the first commander to design field operations around these new weapons, when he attacked the forts on the Tennessee and Cumberland rivers in February 1862.

+>———<+

Rifled artillery alone did not transform the battlefield: the vast majority of casualties still came from rifle fire. But these new guns did have a significant impact on strategy and military engineering. To these developments in infantry firepower and the lethality of artillery must be added two additional technological factors. Although not strictly military in nature, the telegraph and the railroad played a dramatic and unprecedented role in the conflict.

Technically, the telegraph had been widely used in the Crimean War (1854–1856), enabling rapid communication between the commanders on both sides and their distant governments. But the Crimea itself was a small area, and the British, French, and Piedmontese troops all operated independently: even telephones and fax machines would not have changed their inclination to go their own way and fight separate campaigns.

By contrast, in the Civil War the telegraph gave both sides the potential to fight coordinated campaigns, using what amounted to instantaneous transmissions of orders and reports to shape offensive and defensive actions. Given the enormous area over which the war was fought, the telegraph was of much greater importance than in the roughly contemporary European wars.

Both sides could use the telegraph, and did. But Grant actually shaped his concept of warfare around the new device. In so doing, he established yet another link with modern warfare, in which after 1939 the importance of battlefield communications has been increasingly realized. Much of the superiority of the German army in Europe from 1939 to 1941 was based on a rapid and comprehensive communications system that no one else possessed. Similarly, in the late twentieth and early twenty-first centuries, the American army has been able to stay at the forefront of technological innovation in the field of communications, thus maintaining a definite advantage over its enemies in wartime.

As our narrative progresses, we shall see that one measure of Grant's military genius is that he took advantage of this new device and used it to ensure the coordinated and unified offensive campaign that defeated the Confederacy. His predecessors and his opponents by and large did not extract the full potential of the telegraph.

By the 1860s, the railroad was also a commonplace, so it is curious to note that the Civil War was the first war in which rail junctions and routes became important militarily. Again, to a certain extent this is simply a fact of geography. At the risk of some exaggeration, it can be said that in the Confederacy, the north-south transportation system was by water, and the east-west system by rail, while in some key states (central Mississippi and Alabama, for example) the rail system was important in all four directions. The South had to maintain control of its relatively few rail junctions and long-distance lines, while the North, in order to win, not only had to seize them, but needed to protect what it had seized in order to supply its own forces as they moved into the Confederacy.

Properly handled, Southern railroads could have given Confederate armies the enormous military advantage of interior lines of communication, enabling them to shuttle troops back and forth to meet new offensive threats. Basic geography meant that this could have been done faster than the Union could move troops to threaten new offensives. Given that the North had to invade the South and physically occupy its territory, and could not win the struggle by simply winning a major battle, interior lines of communication became much more important than they had in the past.

In fact, the Civil War was the first major war in which the advantage of interior lines of communication became so marked. Acquiring rail lines—the physical track and the rolling stock—became military objectives for both sides. But Grant was the first and for the most part the only commander who shaped offensive operations around railroads. His whole plan for seizing Vicksburg was based on an appreciation of its dependence on the rail lines that intersected in Jackson, Mississippi. Similarly, in his plan for the Battle of Chattanooga, the main objective was not the Confederate rail lines but the railhead behind their right flank.

In fact, to a great extent, this was one reason why neither Grant's opponents nor his superiors really grasped what he was doing. They were all mired in the objectives of an earlier age. Consequently, by the time the Confederates understood Grant's plans, it was generally too late to rectify the situation.

This observation leads us to an important point that often blurs our appreciation of Grant's accomplishments. In discussing the two sides in the Civil War, historians frequently fall into the trap, perhaps unconsciously, of seeing them as wildly mismatched. The North—or so the story goes—had a much larger manpower pool, it had all the industry, and it had all the wealth. The South was smaller and poorer, and as it was primarily an agricultural state, it was completely unprepared for warfare.

This has impacted enormously on our appreciations of Grant, who is frequently seen as being in the same situation as General Bernard Montgomery in North Africa during the Second World War: with such an enormous advantage in equipment and men, how could he help but beat the Germans and their Italian allies? By the same token, all Grant had to do was take advantage of the North's enormous resources—anyone could have won eventually.

On the contrary, the basic parameters favored the Confederacy: the Civil War was very much the South's to lose. Its manpower pool was smaller, but it was considerably more efficient at mobilizing it, the end result being that in terms of actual enlistments, the Union advantage was only about three to two.[11]

Although the weapons of the war were, in comparison with previous wars, new, the basic principle of rifling had been known for three hundred years. It was not conceptually novel, and the basics were easily mastered. It was essentially a very low-tech manufacturing process, and the Confederacy had surprisingly little trouble in equipping what was a relatively enormous army. The South easily had a million men in arms—a figure probably greater than the combined Austrian and Prussian armies deployed in the Seven Weeks War.

In addition, the Union's theoretical advantages were more than offset by the basic strategical problem. In order to win, the Union had to invade the Confederacy, defeat its substantial military force, and physically occupy it. By contrast, in order to win, the South only had to hold out, maintain its territory, and conduct an aggressive defensive war. The word *aggressive* is important here, as advances in artillery meant a passive defense would fail.

The task before the leadership of the Confederacy was not easy. But it was considerably easier than the task that lay before their opponents. The

North bore the burden that it could only win by conducting sustained offensive operations, invading the Confederacy and occupying it. That task would require a great numerical advantage. To the layman, the superiority in numbers mentioned above sounds impressive. But given the forces that would be required to guard supply lines and garrison strongpoints that were taken, the North's numbers were really not sufficient to manage the job properly.

The other problem for the North was that the South mostly consisted of land that European armies had traditionally avoided like the plague. There were certainly places in Europe similar to the American south: the Argonne Forest and the Woëvre Plain in Northern France, for example. But they were considered impracticable places to mount operations. When, in 1914, German officers, who had studied the Civil War carefully, mounted offensives in both places, the French were caught by surprise.

Their surprise was not unreasonable. For centuries professional armies had tried to maneuver so as to fight their battles over relatively clear terrain, and this was true even in the American Revolution, during which the major battles were fought in the relatively cleared agricultural and pastoral regions of the Eastern seaboard. Although there were exceptions in earlier wars on both continents, they were very much exceptions. In order to win, the Union would have to fight in places professional armies had rarely fought before.

It is the measure of Grant's genius that he would be able to fight on this terrain and win, adjusting his plans to the new weaponry, and relying on an army of civilians led by officers often of dubious professional ability.

We think, correctly, of the Civil War as being fought between neighbors, with the two sides sharing a common border. But when the matter is considered properly, the Union would have many of the same difficulties in supply and reinforcement as it invaded the Confederacy that future American armies would have in conducting offensives in Western Europe, Southeast Asia, and the Middle East.

In his successful offensive drives into the Confederacy, Grant managed to square the proverbial circle. He was able to gather forces sufficient to the task and manage to keep them supplied, while at the same time getting them to move quickly, thus keeping the enemy off balance. These two objectives are, to a great extent, contradictory. Armies never think they have enough to support themselves, and sometime they are correct. The necessity for successfully balancing the two objectives was as important in the two Iraq wars as it was in the Civil War.

Fundamentally, these basic principles involved in conducting successful offensive operations have been a constant over the past three centuries of warfare. In war, many things change, but many others stay the same. While this is a truism, the problem is that only successful military leaders can see what has changed and what has not.

Grant had an uncanny instinct for divining the on-the-ground reality. The American military, although it has had its ups and downs, has been remarkably successful at institutionalizing the balance between the need for speed and the need for adequate logistical support, so much so that most of us take it for granted, or assume that nowadays logistics is hardly a factor.

On the contrary, the basic conflict between size of force and maneuverability is now more of a problem than ever before, given the complex logistical requirements of modern armies. The price for failing to solve the problem correctly, for not being able to make the correct tradeoffs, is very high. In 1973 the Soviet Union was remarkably successful in equipping its client-states in the Middle East properly. The armies that the Soviet Union was supplying had made some progress in increasing the tempo of their offensive operations, but not nearly enough to ensure victory. A decade later, the Soviet Union suffered greatly in Afghanistan owing to its inability to juggle the need for fast-moving offensives with adequate support for those operations.

These are all lessons contained in the Civil War. No Union general besides Grant was able to mount successful offensive operations. No Confederate general was able to supply his operations well enough to ensure they were successful. Grant managed to do both, thus establishing that this feat could be accomplished, and setting a very high standard for his successors.

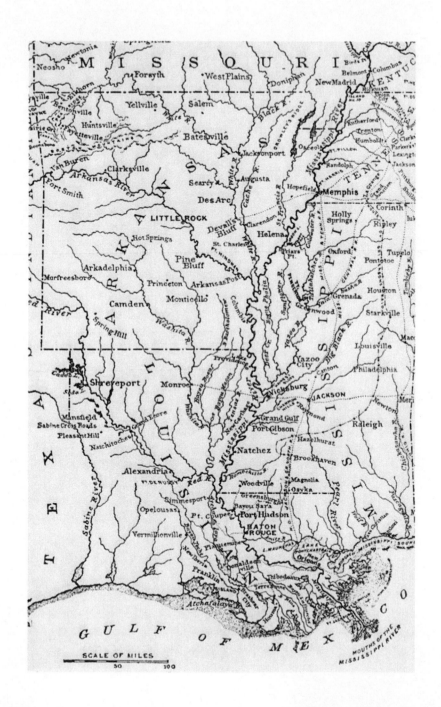

SCALE OF MILES
50   100

CHAPTER 4

A Promising Start

Early Victories

ON APRIL 13, 1861, FORT SUMTER SURRENDERED to the hastily organized Confederates after a heavy bombardment, although the real cause of defeat was insufficient supplies for the garrison. Any hopes of averting a war vanished. The next evening, there was a town meeting in Galena, which Grant attended. As in thousands of other towns and cities, there was a debate. The mayor, although a staunch Republican, still hoped for peace, while the local congressman, Elihu Washburne, argued for war. The crowd, galvanized by an impassioned speech given by a local lawyer, John A. Rawlins, was in no mood to temporize.

Nor was Lincoln, although neither he nor Grant apparently had any real idea of what was in store. They both assumed the South would come to its senses and the war would end quickly. Lincoln called for a mere

75,000 volunteers, who would enlist for a period of only three months. Quotas were set for each state: Illinois was to raise six regiments, and Galena promptly managed two companies. No one in Galena had any military experience whatsoever, and Washburne wanted Grant to be their commander. Had Grant aspired to be an instant hero, he would have marched off to fame and glory at the head of his townsmen.

But real life was different. Grant had deliberately stayed in the peacetime army so he could resign with the rank of captain, an indicator that he had succeeded as an officer. He felt his rank and combat experience entitled him to more than the leadership of a company, and he realized that once he accepted this low level of command, he might end up forever marooned in the same rank he had held when he had resigned. So he declined to lead the company, and agreed only to train them.

At the same time, he believed that his old army colleagues would see a better use for his services. That hope was not fulfilled. His former colleagues simply ignored him. When Grant went to see George McClellan, then a major general and commander of the Ohio militia, McClellan didn't even give him the courtesy of an interview.

It is customary for those of Grant's biographers who deal with this brief period to exaggerate all of this, to attribute the negativity to the allegedly unsavory reputation he had acquired before he resigned. In reality, in spring 1861, those officers who had remained in the army wanted the leadership posts for themselves, and there were hundreds of men who, like Grant, had gone to West Point, done their service, and then resigned—and who now wanted to lead Union troops to glory in what everyone, regardless of their sympathies, believed would be a short war.

An army of 75,000 men simply did not need that many officers, so in those first few weeks of the war, there were more former officers than there were troops. Perhaps more to the point, the governors were giving preference to men who could raise volunteer units on their own.

+>==>==<+

Neither side had any comprehension of how many men would have to be called to arms, but the South had a big advantage. Not having an existing army, they had to create one from scratch. So even though the Confederacy championed state's (and local) rights to the point of near anarchy, its military leadership from the very first was organized by the central government on a national level to be the skeletal basis for a massive force. For the time, this was an astonishing innovation, which would be developed and further systematized by the great continental armies, in which the units mobilized would be organized around a core of officers and men on active duty (or who had recently served). With modifications, this is the system used to this very day: military units, regardless of their classification, are organized around cadres of experienced soldiers.

But Lincoln and the War Department took a different course. The states would raise their own forces of volunteers, figure out how to train and equip them, and decide who their leaders would be. The regular army would remain intact, and lead the Union to victory—just as it had done in the Mexican War. Grant realized this was major blunder. In his own words:

> Seeing those officers who had been educated for the profession of arms, both at school and in actual war, which is a far more efficient training, impressed me with the great advantage the South possessed over the North at the beginning of the rebellion. They had from thirty to forty percent of the educated soldiers of the Nation. They had no standing army, and, consequently, these trained soldiers had to find employment with the troops from their own states. In this way what there was of military education and training was distributed throughout their whole army. The whole loaf was leavened. (*Memoirs*, 144)

He saw right off that the Confederacy would have a major advantage in this regard.

Lincoln's blunder had two entirely predictable results. Inside the regular army, there was a veritable orgy of political maneuvering, as officers struggled to make sure they would be the next great war hero. Meanwhile, the states of the Union basically selected as leaders for their volunteers men with the same desire to serve their country as the volunteers, but often with no qualifications for any sort of command.

Although professional training was no guarantor of success, as both sides struggled to raise enormous armies of civilians and turn them into soldiers, it was a necessity. With one stroke, one simple decision, Lincoln ensured that the Union Army would be stuffed with colonels and generals whose only claim to command was politics.

The other consequence of this decision was bad news for Grant. Regardless of his reputation, since he had retired, Grant's status as the member of a very small elite, graduates of West Point who had seen combat, counted for very little. Presently serving officers wanted all the glory for themselves in what they thought would be a short war.

Initially rebuffed, Grant went to the state capital and put his experience to good use in the governor's office, where his knowledge was appreciated and rewarded. By early May he had begun the task of training a regiment of state volunteers. He did such a good job of it, and the regiment's officers were so impressed, that on June 15, Governor Yates made him a colonel, confirming and making permanent his command of the Seventh District Regiment (a part of the army as the Twenty-first Illinois Volunteers as of June 28).

By that point Grant and his regiment were in Missouri trying to guarantee that the state, a hotbed of Confederate sympathizers, would stay in the Union. It was good training for the men, and for Grant as well: like most junior officers in the Mexican War, he had never had the chance to command a regiment. In fact, there were so few regulars in the Mexican campaigns that even senior officers like Zachary Taylor and Winfield Scott had only a few thousand men under them. By the standards of the old army, a regiment in the field was a major command.

Characteristically, however, when Grant looked back on this period, he remembered not the transition to regimental command, but a psychological revelation. He was pursuing a Confederate officer by the name of Thomas Harris, down by Salt River. Grant deployed his regiment straight toward where Harris was camped, demonstrating a tactic that would become his hallmark: the immediate move to seek out the enemy and attack him.

As we approached the brow of the hill from which it was expected we could see Harris' camp, and possibly find his men ready formed to meet us, my heart kept getting higher and higher until it felt to me as though it was in my throat. I would have given anything to be back in Illinois, but I had not the moral courage to halt. . . . The marks of a recent encampment were clearly visible, but the troops were gone. My heart resumed its place. It occurred to me at once that Harris had been as much afraid of me as I had been of him. (*Memoirs*, 127)

From then on, Grant's philosophy was based on that simple conviction: the enemy was just as frightened, just as terrified, as he was, and probably more so. This revelation accounts for the calmness and courage that characterized his leadership during the war. Victory would go to the side that conquered its fears and continued to fight on.

+⫸━⫷+

Grant was ready to carry the fight to the enemy, and in late June he learned that his refusal to command the local volunteers had paid off. Belatedly, he discovered that the War Department had confirmed him as brigadier general of volunteers, the War Department's designation for all newly recommissioned officers. There's some confusion here, because the appointment list, although not published until late June, had been backdated to May 17, 1861, and apparently no one had bothered to inform Grant, who learned of his status from the newspapers. Given the chaos and confusion in Washington during those first months, the passage of time between the outbreak of the war and Grant's appointment doesn't seem unusual.

Now Grant got a lucky break. The Union Army, still holding to its pre-war organization as a police force, was arranged into departments. In May 1861, the same month that Grant was listed as a brigadier general, Lincoln appointed the famous explorer, John C. Frémont, to head the Department of the West and made him a major general. Frémont was not a successful general. His tenure as commander of the Department of the West was marked by one major engagement, the Battle of Wilson's Creek

(August 10, 1861), notable for being the first battle to see a general killed. Unfortunately for Frémont and the Union, that general was Nathaniel Lyon, whose forces, outnumbered by about two to one, were defeated in a surprisingly bloody engagement in which over a fifth of the Union forces deployed were casualties.[1]

+>——◆——<+

Militarily, Frémont gets short shrift from historians, but he saw one thing clearly, more clearly than anyone else at the time: the key to victory lay in the Mississippi valley. The valley could strategically be divided into three sections, with Frémont's department being responsible for what was initially the most crucial section for the Union.

It would fall to Grant to translate Frémont's idea into a set of military objectives, and it was Grant who would ultimately lead the Union to control over the Mississippi valley, beginning with the upper sections of the river (roughly, north of Tennessee) in the fall of 1861.

Control of this stretch of the river was important. Within this region, at Cairo, Illinois, the Ohio River, which flows in a southwesterly direction from Pittsburg, Pennsylvania, joins the Mississippi. Just before it flows into that river, it makes a southerly loop, beginning at Paducah, Kentucky, along which there are two major splits. The first is the Tennessee River, which flows down south into Georgia. Just upstream, the Cumberland River flows into the Ohio, after bisecting the state of Tennessee. In 1861, all these rivers were navigable (after a fashion) by the flat-bottomed river boats and barges then in extensive use, and Frémont saw that control of this crucial part of the river network was absolutely vital to the Union— and to the Confederacy. Given that Missouri, Kentucky, and Tennessee were all deeply divided states that might secede or stay in the Union, control of the river was important territorially as well.

In retrospect, this seems painfully obvious, but the Union military and civilian leaders were at this point fixated on great battles of annihilation that would result in the capture of Richmond, the new Confederate capital. Geographically, their attention was unalterably fixed on the small area separating the two capitals.

But Frémont was right, and now he dispatched Grant to seize Columbus, Kentucky, a vital strongpoint on the upper Mississippi that was also a railroad head. Before Grant could get going, however, the Confederate general Polk seized the town. The citizens of Kentucky had been sitting on the fence, living in a sort of fantasy world and assuming they could remain neutral. Polk's invasion brought an abrupt halt to this delusion. The legislature joined the Union, and Frémont ordered Grant to protect them.

Grant loaded troops on riverboats at Cairo, and sailed up the Ohio to Paducah, Kentucky. His troops occupied the town, much to the relief of Union loyalists, since Polk's Confederates were literally next door to them. Frémont's orders had been general, Grant's actions specific. He went to Paducah because it was the obvious move to make: the city could block any Confederate movements up the Ohio and into Union heartland.

Stymied in their moves to secure central Kentucky, the Confederates settled on blocking the river at Columbus, which they still occupied. In order to shut off the river to Union traffic they needed both sides of the river, so the Confederates had moved across the river to the little town of Belmont, in theory cutting off the most convenient route connecting southern Missouri with the rest of the Union. Frémont countered by ordering Grant to try to scare the Confederates out of Belmont.

Grant promptly assembled what in modern terms might be called an amphibious task force of abut 12,000 men: five regiments of infantry, a battery of artillery, and a troop of cavalry, all carried on five riverboats and guarded by two ironclad naval vessels. The force steamed down the river, and disembarked on the morning of November 6. Grant landed about three miles north of Belmont. The Confederates, surprised, scattered at the first shots. Finding themselves victorious, Grant's men promptly began celebrating their victory. As well they might: thus far in the war Union victories were rare.

Supported by fire from their positions on the other side of the river, the Confederates promptly crossed it and attempted to cut Grant's forces off from their embarkation point. In this they failed signally. Union troops smashed through the counterattack, got back on their boats, and steamed off.

In 1861, Belmont was, as *Harper's Weekly* reported, "a miserable little village, consisting of a very few houses." It would be easy to paraphrase a similar description of the battle, which was basically nothing more than a successful raid. Neither Ross or Livermore, the two great statisticians of the Civil War, even bother to list Belmont in their exhaustive summaries of engagements, and there were less than 1,500 casualties total.

But in November 1861, the North was desperately short of victories. Belmont was the tenth battle that had been fought. Out of the first nine, only two insignificant engagements could be termed Northern victories: Rich Mountain (July 11, 1861) and Carnifex Ferry (September 10, 1861). The other seven had been Confederate victories, and several of them had been Union disasters, such as First Bull Run (July 21, 1861). So had the engagement right before Belmont, Ball's Bluff (October 21, 1861).

The North needed something it could call a victory, and the Belmont raid provided it. However, there are three other features of the engagement that make it of interest, both in an appreciation of Grant and of modern warfare. Grant had inflicted nearly twice as many casualties on his opponent as his forces had sustained, a ratio 1.9:1, to be exact. Although unremarked, this ratio was in sharp contrast to what had been the case thus far. At Ball's Bluff, for instance, the ratio had been wildly lopsided in favor of the South, with an exchange ratio of nearly three to one (894 Union casualties to 302 Confederate). Perhaps more significantly, nearly half the Union troops engaged were casualties.

It is dangerous to extrapolate trends from these early engagements, and indeed Ball's Bluff was atypical. In general, the difference between Union and Confederate casualties over the course of the war can be measured in only a few percentage points—the basic reason the South lost. But in these early battles, Belmont certainly stands out as a marker of Union combat efficiency—at a time when there weren't any others to speak of.

The key to this level of success was simple: Grant had surprised the Confederate defenders, he had moved quickly against them, and he had brought with him the cavalry and artillery that enabled him to fight off the counter attack that he assumed would be launched. Surprise and speed became Grant's trademark strategy. Again and again he would beat his opponents because he either moved faster than they did, or was somewhere they didn't expect him to be.

This same principle would become one of the trademarks of the American army in future wars, from General John J. Pershing's September 1918 offensive of the American Expeditionary Forces in the Argonne, through the Normandy invasion, and to the amphibious landings at Inchon in the Korean War. Speed and surprise, Grant's constant principles, thus became enshrined in the strategy of the American army.

They still are. In the First Gulf War, the main offensive thrust of the American directed coalition was far to the west of the more developed coastal strip where Saddam Hussein's generals expected it to be. In the Second Gulf War, there was no real air offensive preparatory to the ground offensive: American forces simply attacked. The former offensive achieved surprise in space, the latter in time. Both succeeded however, not simply because of the element of surprise, but because of the speed with which offensive operations developed. The Gulf War offensives were classical Grant operations.

If the explanation for Grant's success at Belmont is simple, the operation itself was complicated, as it involved coordination with the navy. In fact, Belmont was the first instance of a true amphibious operation in modern warfare: previous to that no one had gotten much beyond putting marines (or soldiers) in boats and setting them ashore. They then marched off into battle, the fighting being largely independent of naval aid, and the numbers involved were generally trivial. By comparison, Grant's men disembarked and moved directly into combat. Moreover, in contrast to other abortive Union attempts to transport troops over water, Belmont was a success in this regard as well.

The success of the raid was important in another way. Most everyone in the North felt that the only way to win the war was to invade the Confederacy, defeat its armies, and occupy its territory. This would involve organization, superior maneuvering, and the ability to mount complex offensive operations over large areas. So far, however, the Union had been unable to manage any of this. In the first year of the war, the core of the old regular army, and presumably its outstanding officers, working together in concert with the civilian leadership, had only managed one major battle: Manassas, or the First Battle of the Bull Run, which *Harper's Monthly* repeatedly referred to as a "disaster."[2]

Belmont demonstrated that the North could carry the war to the Confederates and win. Although a minor action, the success was significant, as modern parallel suggests. On August 19, 1942, the British mounted a major raid against the French port of Dieppe in an attempt to gauge how the Germans would react. The short answer was: quickly and brutally. The Dieppe raid was an unqualified disaster at every level. Although the Allies managed to put a modest spin on the fiasco, it presented them with a major problem. In all probability, the only way to win the war was to invade France. The failure of the Dieppe raid suggested this was going to be an extremely difficult proposition. In fact, Dieppe was one reason British Prime Minister Churchill was desperate to land troops anywhere—North Africa, Sicily, Italy, Greece—anywhere but France.

At the end of 1861, the Union was in a roughly similar situation. The disaster of First Bull Run, together with the brutal defeats in smaller engagements, raised the question of whether or not the North could actually prevail in combat. At Belmont, Grant established they could. Curiously, Bull Run was parallel to Belmont in one significant way: in both battles an initial Union success was met by a determined Confederate response, a counterattack. The obvious difference was that in the Virginia battle the Confederate move succeeded, and at Belmont it failed. The reasons aren't hard to find: "Suffice it to say that on the field the confusion of orders and of organization was almost complete," is how one historian describes the Union forces at Manassas.[3] This is precisely the reason why Grant was successful: he was supremely well organized, his orders were clear, and under his direction, the Union troops brushed aside the Confederate counterattack and returned to their boats.

Grant thus possessed both tactical competence and strategic vision. The competence he had now demonstrated. The vision would emerge over the next year. Grant's idea was simple: after securing the upper reaches of the Mississippi River, they would move down the river valley, thus cutting the Confederacy in two and enabling future offensive operations from all sides.

In general, military leaders who had a superior understanding of grand strategy, men like Frémont, were tactically incompetent. Those men who emerged as terrific battlefield commanders rarely had a solid understanding of strategy. The intellectuals, the officers whose knowledge of the art of warfare gave them a fair claim to the leadership, all failed the test when the decisive moment came. This was the great paradox of the Civil War.

Henry Halleck, Grant's commanding general until 1864, was the foremost intellectual in the army, but he was unable either to outmaneuver the Confederates or force them to stand and fight. At the key moment in the Battle of Shiloh, Don Carlos Buell, commander of the Army of the Ohio, became distracted by the numerous stragglers he could see at the rear of the battlefield, and wasted his time trying to get them to fight rather than leading the thousands of fresh troops in his command.

What makes Grant virtually unique, both among Union generals in 1861 and American generals in the great wars that followed, was that he had both the strategic vision of how to win the war and the tactical competence that enabled him to win the battles his strategy required. Pershing and Eisenhower were first rate commanders who led American forces to victory in Europe in two world wars. Neither one of them had any real combat experience at all, much less as a general on the battlefield.

By contrast, it is easy to find examples of men who distinguished themselves in combat as officers, even as divisional commanders, but who were simply unable to function successfully at the higher levels of command. In this respect Grant was different—the only other general who has a similar record is Wellington, and the British general never directed all of his country's armies in a sustained campaign.

Military ineptitude is hardly confined to any one time or place. What makes the Civil War different, however, is that it was the last great war in which the abilities (or lack thereof) of senior commanders played such a decisive role. In that sense the Civil War has much more in common with the Napoleonic wars than with those that came after 1865. At Waterloo, Wellington personally directed his troops, just as Grant did at Shiloh—as did his adversary, Albert Sidney Johnston. Mistakes in command and failures in leadership were thus openly displayed on the battlefield, and with direct consequences.

It is this that makes the Civil War the supreme test of military leadership. We know that Grant was good because he was personally in charge. By 1914, that would no longer be true. A whole set of professional staff officers now existed, insulating the commanders from the actual battlefield. Consequently, their mistakes were often masked by the competence of their field commanders, while their staffs did most of the actual planning.

That is why it is important—to return to the Belmont Raid—to take a close look at Grant's earliest operations, and judge them by their outlines and their results. Put in the proper context, the Belmont Raid sets a pattern, the same pattern that will result in a consistent string of victories; triumphs made all the more impressive by the toughness and professionalism of Grant's opponents.

To recapitulate Grant's strengths: First, there is the speed with which the operation was mounted and the speed with which Grant reacted to the Confederate counterattack; second is the synergy between a strategic view of the war and tactical competence. Grant saw that the upper stretches of the river were strategically important, and he was able to use the right mix of tactics (in this case the use of the navy) to achieve the strategic goal.

Not that Grant's handling of the situation has been thought above reproach. On the contrary, the operation at Belmont has been criticized, the argument being that what happened there indicates Grant had much to learn about the battlefield. The two facts adduced to support this are first, that when the troops broke into the Confederate camp, they started celebrating wildly. The second fact is that Confederate forces launched a counterattack and attempted to cut the Union troops off from their embarkation point.

The behavior of the troops certainly left something to be desired. The moment they reached the Confederate camp, having scattered their enemies, they ran wild, looting and plundering. In a modern army, such behavior is unthinkable, and indicates a serious breakdown of command. But anyone who reads Wellington's dispatches from Spain encounters much the same behavior. "We are an excellent army on parade, an excellent one to fight. . . [but] take my word for it, that either victory or defeat would dissolve us," he wrote, about an army often considered to be one of the best in the world.[4]

Grant had complete confidence that he could land, destroy the enemy, and then leave, regardless of what forces they launched across the river to stop him. In this as in successive judgments, he was perfectly correct. The Confederates didn't stop him, even though they tried. That being the case, it's hard to see how a failed counterattack indicates any sort of tactical failure, particularly given the imbalance in the casualty exchange.

The real conclusion to be drawn from the misbehavior of the troops and the Confederate counterattack is that Grant didn't have any difficulties in rallying the former and in crushing the latter who were trying to stop him from withdrawal. This is the essential Grant: what most leaders would have seen as the chasm of disaster, he saw as simply another hurdle. The pattern will be repeated in later battles, most notably Shiloh.

Moreover, carping about Belmont misses the most important lesson we can draw from it. The record of the Union army units in the 1861 battles, from Big Bethel to Ball's Bluff, are a veritable manual of how not to conduct operations on the battlefield. Belmont reversed the trend.

Having blocked the Confederate attempt to seal off Southern Missouri, Grant now proposed the next logical step to ensure Union control of the upper river: the seizure of the three forts that guarded the Tennessee and the Cumberland rivers as they flowed into the Ohio. The Confederates had built these fortifications because the two rivers extended deep into the heart of the Confederacy, and provided easy access by boat into the southern heartland.

The most formidable, Fort Donelson, was built on a bluff overlooking the Cumberland River. It was protected on one side by a creek that ran into the river; the other landward approaches had steep slopes protected by felled trees and hastily constructed rifle pits. On the Tennessee River, there were two forts. One, Fort Heiman, was a rough copy of Donelson, with a commanding view of the river from a bluff on the west bank. There was one disadvantage to building forts on commanding elevations: if the fort was up high enough, a skillful sailor could slip by directly beneath it, as the fort's guns couldn't be depressed sufficiently to fire directly down to the water.

A fort was built on the other side of the river, so that gunners could fire directly at vessels trying to slip beneath Heiman. This was Fort Henry. Given the short distance between the two rivers at this point (less than twelve miles) any attack would be a complicated affair. Henry and Heiman would have to be attacked simultaneously.[5] Mounting a siege would be dangerous, because troops at Donelson could attack the besiegers from the rear, and the same thing would apply if Donelson was attacked first.

But Grant was convinced that a coordinated effort involving ironclads (armored naval vessels) and the army could take all three forts. He went to Henry Halleck, the new commander of the Department of the Missouri (Frémont having been sacked for emancipating the slaves), and pitched his plan. Halleck was hardly interested.

For Halleck, the forts and the upper river were simply a nuisance. In his view wars were won by accumulating an overwhelming force and occupying territory inch by inch. This was the lesson he had absorbed from his study of European wars and the conclusions that had been drawn from them. Like most such lessons, then and subsequently, this one was wrong, but Halleck was neither the first nor the last general to get things backwards.

Although Halleck felt he was an expert on theories of war, he had missed the important revolutions in gunnery and warfare that made Grant's plan not only feasible, but imperative. Both sides were developing a new type of riverboat that would turn America's vast inland waterway network into a series of military expressways. Steam power made it possible to propel a vessel without sails, which in turn meant that the vessel could have a protected superstructure, and indeed the great riverboats that were increasingly seen along the Mississippi were basically floating houses. Steam also gave them the power to move against the formidable currents of these great rivers, and the absence of any sort of oceanic weather—waves, tides, great storms—meant that the vessels could have a shallow enough draught to operate in low-lying water.

Covering the superstructure with iron plates to protect its crew and its guns was an obvious step, and by the end of 1861 both sides were building ironclad river boats. Such vessels would eventually revolutionize naval warfare, but the great navies of the world were all blue-water affairs, and figuring out how to construct an ironclad ocean-going warship that wouldn't sink in the first real storm was not a trivial matter.

Initially, there was not much need for ironclads. Ocean-going vessels could stand far enough out to sea to make them reasonably tough targets for fortress gunners. And up until the advent of the rifled gun, whose impact was only just beginning to be perceived in 1861, properly constructed fortifications would enable the gunners to operate in relative security, while a solid hit from one of their weapons could disable a wooden ship or even sink it. Besides, navies didn't build fleets to battle forts: they built ships to fight other ships.

The new rifled artillery, although in short supply, changed that equation. In theory it gave both attacker and defender a new lethality. Assuming both sides were armed with equivalent rifled guns, it would tip the scales dramatically in favor of the fort. Mounting iron plates on the ship was an attempt to even the balance. This was particularly important for river boats, since the gunners in the forts would be firing at such short ranges. And the technical problems of increasing the weight of the vessel were much less complicated. Seaworthiness—the ability to ride out the gale-force winds and fifty-foot waves of the Atlantic Ocean—was not an issue. Any barge could be upgraded, any steamboat used as the model. As a result, the expertise required was widely available: a sizeable fleet of river-going ironclads was built in Saint Louis and river ports further north.

In the short time since the start of the war, Confederate engineers hadn't been able to construct fortifications that would withstand serious bombardments, or renovate existing structures to a higher standard. So the fortifications on the Cumberland and Tennessee rivers were—for perhaps only a limited time—basically obsolete, although at Donelson the batteries were on two levels (this enabled gunners to fire low, and hopefully hit their target at or below the waterline).

Unlike Halleck, Grant and the local naval commander, Andrew Hull Foote, saw quickly enough that ironclads armed with rifled guns could wreak havoc on such fortifications. Each of the half-dozen vessels being built locally for river warfare was therefore armed with three or four rifled guns and seven or eight smoothbore cannons. The combination of ironclad riverboat and the rifled gun was one of those technological synergies that could, in theory, revolutionize one part of warfare.

The technology was simple and available; but speedy action was important. Although it is customary to begin any discussion of the Civil War by enumerating the industrial superiority of the Union over its new adversary, the advantage is grossly overstated. For the first part of the war, the Confederacy could buy whatever it needed abroad, as the blockade that secretary of the Navy Gideon Welles had instituted to strangle the Confederacy's import-export trade would need years to become effective—the Union simply didn't have the navy required to mount a blockade of much consequence.

As time passed, then, the Confederates would equip themselves with rifled guns, strengthen their fortifications, and present the Union with defenses that would be difficult to overcome. But when Grant presented his plan, Halleck had no idea what he was talking about, and dismissed the whole idea as crazy. Halleck intended to fight the war according to sound principles derived from his extensive studies of Napoleon, and he regarded Grant as wild, uncouth, and of dubious moral character.

Undaunted, Grant got Foote, the naval commander, to go pitch the plan once more. When Foote went to make the case, he was treated differently. He was a naval officer and could complain to Secretary Welles, whose opinion of Halleck was scathing, no less for being absolutely accurate. According to Welles, Halleck "originates nothing, anticipates nothing. . . . takes no responsibility, plans nothing, suggests nothing, is good for nothing."[6]

It's always easy to justify doing nothing, and it was here that Halleck excelled. Left to his own devices, Halleck would probably have remained in Saint Louis forever—and kept Grant there as well—but a new threat reared its head. Halleck perceived that his chances for advancement might be blocked by the appointment of one of now Commander in Chief George McClellan's proteges, Brigadier General Don Carlos Buell.

Lincoln was particularly concerned about the situation in Kentucky and Tennessee, perceiving correctly that the citizens of both states—and particularly in the eastern portions—were Union sympathizers. His idea, which was vague and unmilitary, was for the army to give them support in more or less the same way that Grant had when he had moved on Paducah, Kentucky. Buell had a better idea, which was to get to Nashville and capture it. Confederate General Albert Sidney Johnston didn't have enough men to defend all of Tennessee, and, as we have seen, he was planning to conduct his main defense at the river forts.

Halleck could see the situation clearly enough: Lincoln was desperate for someone to do something, had issued an order requiring offensive operations, and now a dangerous rival was on the move to his east, a rival who moreover was backed by a man Halleck couldn't stand—George McClellan. He was confronted with the worst possible fate: competition from his own side. The thing to do was to let the two brigadier generals, Buell and Grant, compete with each other. So Halleck, ever sensitive to his career prospects, suddenly changed his mind. Grant was ordered to take the forts.

For most officers this would have been a formidable task. When Johnston had taken over command of the Confederate forces in the West, he had determined to make the best fight possible for the upper Confederacy, and had concentrated a force at Donelson, which eventually came to about 21,000 men, with a decent complement of artillery. For early 1862, this was a sizeable force: at First Bull Run, the Union forces had less than 29,000 men.[7] An assault on the forts would therefore have to be the largest offensive operation the North had undertaken since the July disaster, and in fact about as many Union soldiers were involved.

Again, Grant proved himself adept at what was, for the time, an enormous logistical feat. Charles Smith, an aging senior officer who had been Grant's West Point commandant, would land on the west bank and attack Fort Heiman, while Grant's other divisional commander, John McClernand, would land near Henry. All this would be coordinated with Foote's gunboats, so Grant was planning a doubly ambitious undertaking: two simultaneous attacks that would have to be coordinated with the navy.

In Foote, Grant found a senior officer who was as keen to move quickly as he was, and competent to boot. It would be a unique experience. And here it paid off. Grant's men began landing on February 4, 1861. On the morning of the sixth, Foote's gunboats began shelling Fort Henry, whose defenders discovered that Colonel Adolphus Heiman, faced with Smith's division, had simply abandoned the fort and withdrawn his men to Donelson.

Given the superior range and accuracy—and iron plates—of Foote's squadron, there was little the gunners at Henry could do to stop the guns of the ironclads. Their position had been designed to work in unison with the guns in Heiman, not independently. By the afternoon, the Confederate commander, Lloyd Tilghman, decided his position was hopeless, and evacuated the fort, leading most of the garrison, about 3,000 men, overland to Fort Donelson.

From a layperson's point of view, the decision is easy to understand: it was either evacuate the forts or stay there and fight on to the bitter end—and defeat. Militarily, of course, this was also exactly the right thing to do. Tilghman and Heiman were good officers who had been at West Point. They felt their first obligation was the welfare of their men, so they abandoned their positions. But in so doing, they opened up the Tennessee river to Union forces—in theory, all the way over to Muscle Shoals, Alabama.

Grant's success was, therefore, not due to a mistake made by his opponents. It came about first because he was able to plan and execute an ambitious maneuver, and second because he and Foote understood how the combination of ironclads and rifled guns had shifted the balance. The withdrawals were exactly what one would expect from professional soldiers of the period. The third reason for Grant's success is the great imponderable: great generals are not just smarter than their opponents, they're luckier. And the luck is generally due to superior intuition.

Napoleon had wanted his generals to have this quality. But intuition is a talent that can't be taught. You either have it or you don't. And Grant had it. At some level he simply knew that his opponents would quit the fight, and this belief (or insight, or intuition) enabled him to brush aside all the potential disasters that could have taken place. Where Halleck—and many other Union generals—could only see the potential for disaster, Grant saw victory.

+⟫━━⟪+

Now that Grant had taken Henry and Heiman, Donelson was isolated. No one was going to come to the aid of the defenders; no one would attack the Union troops from behind. Within a week Grant and Foote were on the Cumberland river and the attack had begun.

There were no less than three Confederate brigadier generals at Donelson: John Floyd, Gideon Pillow, and Simon Buckner, each with his own ideas on how to conduct a defense of the fort. Floyd, who had seniority, was in overall command, while both Buckner and Pillow were outside the fort, covering the approach to the batteries. This was a strong defensive position. The Confederates were entrenched and confident, and a direct assault would be needed if the fort were to be taken without a protracted siege. Grant would be the first commander to direct a frontal attack against an entrenched enemy armed with rifled muskets.

Initially the defenders did well enough. The initial purpose of the advance of McClernand and Smith was to ascertain the nature of the landscape surrounding the fort and then seal it off. Today, when we look at the carefully tended and cleared battlefields of the war, it is easy to forget that in 1861 they were mostly underbrush and forest. Nor were there any topographical maps available. The only way to understand the contours of the ground was to explore it in person.

McClernand was slow to cover his section of the front, thus establishing, or perhaps solidifying, a failing that would never really be remedied. Grant would spend the next four years trying to get his generals to move more quickly. McClernand's troops had been steadily drawing fire as they struggled through the brush. The next morning, assuming that the lack of musketry from the positions he could see meant that they had been abandoned or were lightly held, McClernand now made another serious error: his men mounted a frontal attack, uphill, against the position held by Heiman and his Tennesseans. Given the distances involved, as well as the elevations, this was a textbook example of how the new technology of the rifled musket rendered a direct frontal attack on a broad front suicidal.

Meanwhile, on the river, Foote's sailors were quickly finding out that the Confederate fort on the Cumberland was a different matter entirely from Henry and Heiman. Its batteries had a commanding view of the river.

What Foote was now discovering was that in river warfare, naval vessels lost the ability to maneuver that they had on the ocean: rivers were too narrow to give them the mobility that was crucial to their safety. In order to unleash his firepower, Foote had to close within five hundred yards. At that range the batteries in the fort could hardly miss, nor did they. Two of his four boats were seriously disabled, and the flotilla withdrew down the river. To add to the general woe, on the day of Foote's attack, the weather had turned nasty: freezing rain, mixed with sleet and snow.

Grant had no real control over Foote, nor was he able to do much about McClernand. What he was able to do, however, was of great importance. Now that the Union troops had managed to identify the roads and paths leading to the fort, he could see that the main route back to the Confederacy—the road that led to Charlotte—was the only practicable route in and out of the fort. Prudently, Grant had left Lew Wallace back at Fort Henry, to prevent Floyd from shuttling troops back and forth. Now that he had Donelson sealed off, he moved Wallace's division to Donelson to block the road.

Despite their initial success, when the three Confederate generals learned that their escape route had been sealed, they immediately resolved that the only course of action was to fight their way through the Union lines to safety. Thus far, everything had gone in their favor. It would seem rather obvious that the defenders of a fort under siege could expect to be surrounded, so why their discovery precipitated the Confederate decision is hard to fathom.

⊹━━⊹

Tilghman and Heiman had begun their ruin of Johnston's defensive plans for Donelson by hastily abandoning the forts on the Tennessee. Now three more of his officers would finish the job. In account after account of the

Confederacy, we are told of their courage, their commitment to a cause clearly lost. And there is no doubt that the ordinary soldiers paid again and again with their blood for that cause. About the resolution of their officers, the same cannot be said. Here on two separate occasions their immediate response to a serious offensive was to hightail it back to safety.

Floyd directed Buckner and Pillow to mount a general attack. Whatever the justification for the decision, it was an invitation to disaster. Not only would it commit the garrison to making a direct frontal attack, but it would abandon the only defensive position the Confederacy had in the area.

Grant, like any competent officer, expected that the defenders, buoyed by their initial success, would now dig in for the long haul, and had gone aboard Foote's badly damaged warship to urge him to enter the fray once more, this time coordinating it with the ground forces. Grant was surprised by the Confederate attack only because it made no sense—unless one assumed that the Confederate leaders had panicked and were resolved to cut and run. That insight explains Grant's subsequent actions and his self confidence that the shaken officers around him found remarkable.

McClernand had managed to bungle the defense of the road, and Wallace had done little to help him. By the time Grant got on shore, what should have been an inconclusive firefight had turned into a rout. Given competent leadership and decently trained troops, the Confederate attack would have been suicidal, but ten months into the war, the North had hardly any of the former and very little of the latter. On the Charlotte road, Grant had neither one.

This was, in fact, one of the very few times in the war when Grant's generally calm and reticent manner vanished, to be replaced not by fear or anxiety, but simple anger. As Lew Wallace, who was there, records it:

> His face flushed slightly. With a sudden grip he crushed the papers in his hand. But in an instant these signs of disappointment or hesitation—as the reader pleases—cleared away. In his ordinary quiet voice he said, addressing himself to both officers, "Gentlemen, the position on the right must be retaken." With that he turned and galloped off.[8]

Notice the imperative verb: the order left no room for misunderstanding. Nor was there any reason for him not to be confident. He had plenty of troops on the ground, and the Confederate victory was not sustainable. The mere fact that the Confederate soldiers had attempted to break out of the fort (dead and captured soldiers had full knapsacks, suggesting their intentions) was strong evidence that his opponents had panicked and thrown in the towel. Moreover, from his own experiences, he knew that at this stage of an engagement, success was often fatal. As he had seen firsthand at Belmont, success could lead to disorganization, confusion, and overconfidence.

━━━◆━━━

In the case of the three Confederate generals, it also led to a quarrel. Pillow, whose men had routed their opponents, fired off a message to Johnston saying that he had destroyed the Union forces and won a great victory, thus trying to turn his very real failure—his abandonment of the fort—into a success. At the same time, Pillow got into a bitter tiff with Buckner, claiming that he had failed to support his success, and ordered Buckner to launch a hot pursuit of the retreating enemy.

Buckner, the only West Pointer in the group, had in mind a deliberate evacuation, and wanted to delay. Floyd, who at this point was totally overwhelmed both by the situation and his juniors, did nothing. So Buckner was forced to launch an attack in pursuit of an allegedly routed soldiery. Meanwhile, Pillow launched the bulk of the garrison in what he imagined to be a hot pursuit, only to run squarely up against a Union counterattack—with predictable results.

In the meantime, Grant had ordered Charles Smith, the only competent divisional commander he had, to attack the fort directly, since it was clear that the bulk of the garrison was chasing down the Charlotte road. Here was the second instance in which a direct frontal attack could succeed: when the defenders were so outnumbered that they could only kill a small percentage of the attackers before they were overwhelmed.

Moreover, in this as in many other engagements, the attackers were not advancing over open ground. There was plenty of cover, owing both to irregularities of the terrain and to the timber strewn over the area. So Smith's attack succeeded. His men seized the rifle pits that formed the main defensive position on the land side of the fort.

By this time Buckner and Pillow, far from breaking out, had been repulsed, and driven back to the fort. And when Buckner tried to storm the old defensive positions, he was again repulsed. The Confederates were now thoroughly demoralized, and decided to give up. No better evidence of Grant's original epiphany back in Missouri could be found: his officers were scared and nervous, but so was the enemy. Victory went to the side that refused to panic at the first serious reverse. Thus did Grant lay the groundwork for what is today taken as one of the basic points of combat training. To use the phrase of a twentieth-century French general, "Every war has its routs and one must deal with them calmly, sensibly, and without delay."[9]

Before the war Floyd had served under President Buchanan as Secretary of War, and in 1861 he was under indictment for embezzling government funds. He took the reasonable position that if he surrendered the United States would try him as a common criminal, and so he took advantage of his seniority, hiked upstream, and caught a steamboat for Nashville. Pillow escaped as well. Buckner, the only one of the three generals with any claim either to competence or integrity, was thus stuck with the unhappy duty of surrendering the command that Floyd and Pillow had managed to throw away.

Bedford Forrest, the Confederate cavalry officer, simply assembled his men and made a run for it during the night, which raises an interesting point: had the senior commanders shown half the ingenuity in holding their position that they demonstrated in fleeing from it, things might have taken a different turn.

Back in Saint Louis, Halleck—who had not heard of Grant's victory—was in despair. Everyone knew that for a siege to be successful there had to a ratio of five soldiers attacking to every one soldier defending. Grant had hardly any more men than his opponents. He was caught between two fortified positions. Halleck's advice was to dig in and do nothing. When Henry and Heiman fell, he repeated his injunction, adding helpfully that Grant could make use of slave labor to entrench, and that he was sending him shovels. As though there were cotton plantations lining the banks of the Cumberland and the Tennessee!

At the same time, Halleck was feverishly mounting his own campaign. Not against the nominal enemy commander, Albert Johnston, but against Grant. By the time Buckner was forced to surrender Donelson, Halleck had offered Grant's command to every officer still breathing, beginning with Ethan Allen Hitchcock, an aging veteran of the Mexican war. He was so desperate he even volunteered to hand the whole affair over to Don Carlos Buell. That way, when the expedition ended in a fiasco, he would have removed himself from the chain of command. Halleck was no shirker at shirking responsibility.

Alas, there is no reliable witness to record his reaction when the news reached him that the Confederates had fled, the remainder of the garrison had surrendered, and Grant had won the first Union victory of any consequence whatsoever (although subsequently the estimated size of the defeated Confederate force was minimized), Floyd had at least 17,000 men under his command, and probably about 21,000—nearly as many men as had fought at First Bull Run. Grant demanded that the unfortunate Buckner surrender unconditionally, thus creating an instant legend and nickname. At least 12,000 soldiers, maybe as many as 15,000, marched out of the fort when Buckner capitulated.[10]

Despite the heavy fighting in the three attacks, Grant had only about 2,300 casualties of all sorts, while the Confederates had suffered roughly 3,000. Aside from the fact that the loss of the forts had completely wrecked Albert Johnston's defensive strategy for the northwest Confederacy, Grant's victory was definitive on its own. The Northern press went wild. Grant was the man of the hour, and rightly so: the war had now been raging for almost a year and this was the first large Union victory. And since the newspapers had touted Belmont as a major feat, Grant now appeared to be the only Union general who could beat the rebels.

Behind every successful general stand a phalanx of jealous colleagues and subordinates anxious to make it clear that someone else was really responsible for his success—or that it was entirely a fluke, and completely undeserved. Halleck, rather shrewdly, was trying to play both sides of this. It had crossed his mind that as Grant's superior, these successes would make him look good. So while he plotted against Grant behind his back, to Grant's face Halleck was the properly grateful superior.

In doing so, Halleck played to Grant's one great flaw. Like many successful men, Grant was entirely too trustful of those he worked with, assuming that their motivations were like his. In Halleck's case, Grant didn't discover the truth about the general's intrigues until after the war. But even during the war, he was entirely too patient and forgiving of inept commanders like McClernand and sly deconstructionists like Lew Wallace. And afterwards, when he became president, this misplaced trust got him into difficulty after difficulty.

That being noted, however, the idea that these early victories were not so great as they seemed—and that Belmont was almost a disaster—are misrepresentations of the chaos of the battlefield. Although the Union troops would acquire experience while in battle, in November 1861 they had very little and were essentially a mob of civilians with guns and uniforms. Their officers, almost entirely civilians themselves, were no more able to maintain or restore order than the men were to keep it. The troops would degenerate into a mob whether they won or lost—just as Wellington had observed about the peninsular army.

Both at Belmont and Donelson, Grant was forced to intervene personally and salvage the situation. The argument that this intervention suggests some tactical deficiency on his part, that he was forced to it, owing to some error of judgment, is simply unfounded. So too with the argument made by Grant's detractors that the basic plan to take the forts came from others, that although Grant was a decent commander, the real architect of victory was Halleck or even Frémont.

Such criticisms—often made in discussing military operations—neglect the principle, quoted earlier, that the basis of strategy is common sense. The problem the Union faced was not trying to figure out what needed to be attacked, it was figuring out how to carry out a successful operation against the forts. To move the point forward: everyone knew that in order for the United States to defeat Germany in the Second World War, it would have to invade Europe. The contributions of Generals Eisenhower and Montgomery, working together, was to decide on a given place (Normandy) and then to plan an operation sufficiently powerful to succeed.

+➤═➤+

There are three factors that make these early campaigns of interest. First, like Napoleon, Wellington, and von Moltke the Elder, Grant believed in moving directly to the attack. However, like the latter two generals, Grant's idea was to force his opponents to counterattack once his initial moves had threatened them. Grant would use this strategy time and again.

Grant's moves at the forts would be repeated in the Vicksburg campaign, particularly the probing actions that sealed off the city. Given his resources in both situations, this was no mean feat, and not nearly so obvious as it sounds when summarized: large fortified areas are very difficult to seal off completely. They usually leak. Grant's moves in both places thus establish a pattern: they show how adept he was at turning the terrain to his advantage. This leads to the second point: Grant's mastery of geography. Given the terrain around the forts, and later at Vicksburg, there simply weren't that many routes that could be used, but Grant made the most of the terrain and made it work to his advantage.

Third, like those two great adversaries, Napoleon and Wellington, Grant was a master of improvisation. He knew that no plan survived the first gunshot; you had to put together specific moves on the battlefield in real time while the battle was going on. "You engage, then you wait and see," was how Napoleon put it.[11] What he found unnecessary to add was that when the moment to respond came, the response had to be made with lightning speed. For all Halleck's alleged knowledge of Napoleon, he never understood the master's most basic axiom. Grant did.

Without speed, surprise became simply a minor advantage. The ability to exploit surprise quickly and decisively—always Grant's objective—would become an integral component of American military doctrine. What made the Inchon assault in the Korean War so successful was how quickly American forces exploited the advantage of the surprise assault far behind enemy lines. What made the American ground offensive in the second Iraq war so successful was that it moved so quickly, overrunning defensive positions before they could be organized. Grant made clear that it was not enough simply to respond quickly: the response had to be so powerful that it simply rolled over the soldiers on the other side, making them choose between flight, surrender, and death.

CHAPTER 5

Enemies in the Rear

HAVING WON THE FIRST REAL UNION VICTORY since the start of the war, Grant now aimed to move south. The reason was simple: now that his whole defensive strategy to guard the entrance to the western Confederacy with the forts on the two rivers had gone downstream, Confederate general Albert Sidney Johnston decided he had no choice but to abandon the greater part of Tennessee and regroup in northern Mississippi.

Already, as Grant was reorganizing his forces on the Cumberland, word came that Clarksville, only a short distance up the river, had been abandoned. Shortly thereafter, Grant learned that Nashville had been abandoned as well, and the Confederates had retreated all the way down to Murfreesboro.

In 1861, Tennessee was an important resource to whichever side controlled it. It was not simply because of the rivers, which provided avenues for the transport of supplies and for attack by water. The sympathies of its citizens were divided, as was the case in most of the border states. As a relatively populous area, it potentially could supply the Confederacy with at least 50,000 recruits. Strategically, whoever had control of the central and western portions of the state was in an excellent position to move north into neighboring Kentucky, or south into Mississippi.

Given that the Union was going to have to invade the Confederacy, Tennessee was therefore more important to the North than to the South. And as Grant had seen in Missouri and Kentucky, those citizens loyal to the Union, or likely to support the cause, needed a show of Union force for protection and reassurance. The Confederate retreat was therefore a golden opportunity to advance the Union cause in a critical area, one that would substantially hamper any Confederate ideas of future offensive operations. In 1863 the Confederacy did just that, forcing the Union to contest parts of Tennessee all over again.

Grant now had 36,000 men. The obvious move was to occupy middle and western Tennessee and then advance into Mississippi before Johnston could organize his defense. The loss of the forts was as demoralizing to the South, who had hitherto seen itself as winning one victory after another, as it was a tonic for the North. When he had fired Frémont for emancipating the slaves in Missouri, Lincoln had attempted to maintain the notion that a reconciliation was possible without a great social upheaval in the South. By March 1862 there had been relatively few soldiers killed in action. If there was another bold move, something that gave everyone the impression that the Union forces had momentum and were unstoppable, the war might come to a quick conclusion. The key to victory in 1862 was exactly what Frémont had argued it to be in 1861: seizing control of the Mississippi River Valley, and particularly the fortress of Vicksburg.

Grant saw that the next step, having opened up the rivers to Union ironclads, was to drive on Corinth, Mississippi, an important railroad junction just south of the Tennessee state line. At Corinth, the railroad coming up from the port of Mobile and the Alabama coast intersected the main east-west line that ran from the Atlantic all the way to Memphis, Tennessee. Seize Corinth and Memphis would be cut off from the rest of the Confederacy. Seize Memphis and the river would be clear all the way down to Vicksburg.

The railroad that went south from Corinth formed a convenient route through the center of the state of Mississippi. Grant reckoned that once he had seized Corinth, he could move his force down the railroad to Jackson. As Vicksburg was almost due west of that city, he would then cut the city off from its supply base, advance along the rail line, and attack the city from the rear.

Grant's plan was based on a realistic appreciation of terrain, a perfect understanding of how the existence of railroads had changed military objectives, and on a shrewd analysis of the state of the Confederate armies in the west. The only practicable north-south route through Mississippi was along the main rail line: the terrain along the western part of the state was almost impassable in all but the driest months of the summer. The only way to attack Vicksburg was from the east, and the best way to ensure that both Vicksburg and Memphis would fall to the Union was to cut of the railroads connecting them to with the rest of the Confederacy. That in turn meant taking Corinth and Jackson.

After the fall of the forts, Albert Sidney Johnston had to reorganize his forces. He was universally recognized as one of the South's best generals, but a month after Grant's victory at Donelson, he had only assembled a force of 40,000 men. Grant already had nearly that many soldiers concentrated and ready to move. These were men who had been in combat and won. In February 1862, Grant's plan was eminently feasible. As one Austrian military expert remarked in his analysis of Helmuth von Moltke's three short and victorious wars, "Prussia has conclusively demonstrated that the strength of an armed force derives from its *readiness.* . . . A ready army is twice as powerful as a half-ready one."[1]

The idea that the Mississippi river was vital to both sides, and particularly to the Confederacy, was not a notion restricted to Ulysses S. Grant. Southern generals in the west were quite conscious of its importance, and were moving rapidly to bolster their forces and block any further incursions. A quick advance to Corinth was vital.

Grant's ideas on how to proceed fell on deaf ears. Back in Saint Louis, Halleck responded with great alacrity to Grant's news of Donelson— though not to Grant. Halleck never congratulated him, and didn't even respond to his report on the victory. But he immediately flew into action with the War Office. The triumph was his, and entitled him to overall command of all the armies in the west, he told the War Department. To that end, he requested that Brigadier Generals Ulysses S. Grant, Don Carlos Buell, and John Pope all be promoted to major general.

To compensate for his energy in advancing his career, Halleck peremptorily told Grant to stay where he was, thus committing one of the greatest blunders of the war: Albert Johnston was in dire need of time to get organized and Halleck's orders served him time on a silver platter. Johnston's forces were swelling by the day, and he was pondering how to redeem the situation and wrest Tennessee back from the Union army. Halleck now handed over the initiative to Johnston and ordered Grant not to move.

⊹━══━⊹

As Halleck would be Grant's superior for most of the war, it is worth explaining the underlying basis for this and future actions. Before 1861, Halleck had acquired a reputation as one of the army's foremost military theorists and intellectuals. When the fighting started, he assumed that his knowledge of warfare vastly exceeded that possessed by anyone else. Halleck believed that modern wars were won not by fighting battles, but by cautious maneuvers that occupied territory. Actual fighting was to be avoided unless you had an overwhelming advantage in numbers.[2]

Halleck was therefore horrified by Grant's aggressiveness, which contradicted the theories that in his view defined how wars could be won. In other words, Grant had been twice lucky (at Belmont and the forts) but it was reckless luck, and if he continued unchecked, disaster would ensue. There was an important corollary to this idea: Grant didn't know any better, didn't understand the basics of military theory, and that was why he was bent on charging off and provoking a battle.

Halleck was hardly the only Union general to believe that the notion of a battle was old fashioned and unnecessary, that those who understood military theory would be able to prevail by applying their ideas to actual campaigns. The postulations of the theorists of this generation had little basis in how wars had been fought in the last hundred years. In the twentieth century, the same mistake would be repeated. Theorists would look at warfare and from these events they would deduce certain principles. But, when the next war began, their theories would quickly be proved wrong. The Italian airpower theorist, Giulio Douhet, argued, for example, that air defenses were useless: there was no way to keep bombers from getting through. The example of Dresden hardly needs to be cited to prove that this idea was completely wrong.

Grant's disdain for theory, his determination to fight wars to win, regardless of how this determination contradicted intellectual notions, placed him in the mainstream of military thinking. In the nineteenth century, the French and German military theorists worshipped by American officers like Halleck were mostly ignored by the officers of those two countries. When France declared war on Prussia in July 1870, the aim of Helmuth von Moltke the Elder, the great chief of staff of the Prussian Army, was simple: move into France and destroy their armies in a series of great battles of annihilation, just as he had done earlier with Denmark and Austria. The senior French commanders, all distinguished veterans of Crimea and Algeria, were only too glad to oblige him. It was as if Halleck and Buell were trapped in some intellectual backwater.

There is also a dark side to all of this. Halleck certainly believed that he was right and Grant was wrong, that he was the great theorist and Grant was ignorant. So he subsequently interpreted every action of Grant's in the worst possible light. But when Halleck's behavior towards Grant throughout the war is examined, there is another interpretation as well: Halleck was mostly interested in advancing his own career, and to this end devoted most of his energies to vanquishing his rivals, both actual (McClellan) and potential (Grant). Like any shameless careerist, he was amazingly successful, but whether his motives were pure or impure, the net result was to prolong the war.

Without meaning to, Halleck was given an assist from President Lincoln. Grant saw the importance of Tennessee, as did the president. Where the two men differed was that Grant realized that the strategically vital part of the state was the area stretching from Nashville to Memphis, and that the far eastern part of the state, mountainous and much less prosperous, had no real military value. But Lincoln saw that part as important, chiefly because the area contained numerous Union supporters. His motives were good, but his grasp of the actual situation was imperfect.

Lincoln, fixated on how to take eastern Tennessee, inadvertently managed to empower Halleck, giving him free rein in the Mississippi River valley and western Tennessee, which in turn meant that Halleck was free to control Grant by nailing him to the spot.

Meanwhile, Buell and his Army of the Ohio was slowly moving south. Buell, like Halleck, eschewed the actual fighting of battles, and his progress was glacial. Buell and Halleck agreed that Grant's recklessness meant that he would be tied up besieging Fort Donelson for months, and Buell had agreed to send General William Nelson and his Fourth Infantry Division west to reinforce the siege that they both confidently predicted would go on through the spring.

By the time Nelson and his men arrived, the victory had been won. Grant suggested to General Nelson that he could accomplish something useful. He could steam upriver and occupy Nashville. Grant couldn't, because Halleck had told him to stay put, but as Nelson reported to Buell, Halleck had no authority over him.

Nelson promptly seized Nashville, which had been abandoned, just as everyone said. When Buell arrived on the outskirts of the city, he was furious. He was convinced that Johnston was lurking nearby, ready to pounce on with an enormous army and destroy them all. Like Halleck, Buell had theories to support his direction of the Army of the Ohio that he felt Johnston had contradicted in his seizure of Nashville.

＋＞－＝＜＋

But there is a simpler explanation, one that is necessary to outline in order to appreciate why Grant was so good at his profession. In professional armies of any sort, peacetime generals are often averse to engaging in combat. We could even call this timidity. Both in 1870 and again in 1914, many French generals were extremely reluctant to move into situations that would involve fighting. In May 1940, the British Expeditionary Force in France simply withdrew in the face of the rapid German advance, and only began to fight when British leaders realized the necessity of defending their evacuation port. In many instances, faced with a serious attack, the response of the enemy army is simply to quit, as was the case in both Iraq campaigns.

"Delay in war is fatal," Napoleon had said. But it is also understandable, because fear is a universal affliction. It is also not susceptible to any easy cure. On February 27, 1862, Grant went to Nashville to try to persuade Buell that Johnston was far to the south, and that far from commanding an enormous army, he was trying to piece together a fairly small one.

But Buell, who hadn't even entered the city, and was sitting across the river, was adamant. He believed that Johnston was going to swoop down on them at any moment. In fact, Buell demanded reinforcements from Grant to fight off the vast Confederate juggernaut that would descend on him shortly. As it turned out, Johnston's scattered force were moving in the other direction at that precise moment. Part of the problem, one that Grant would encounter over and over again, was that although only a minority of West Pointers had gone over to the Confederacy, that minority was the cream of the crop. So much so that in later years, when German Chancellor Otto von Bismarck asked Grant if he thought that a larger standing army might have prevented the war, Grant said no: " . . . if we had had a large regular army, as it was then constituted, it might have gone with the South."[3]

There is a certain ambiguous, oracular, quality to the remark, as is often the case with Grant. What he meant was that at the start of the war, those officers who went with the South were among the most senior and the most respected in the army. In the pre-war military, based on regiments of less than 1,000 men and only a handful of officers, the influence of any one colonel or general was quite limited. Had the army been larger, these men would have been commanding tens of thousands of men and hundreds of officers: they would have been even more influential. When Secession loomed, Winfield Scott, the overall commander of the Union army, wanted someone younger to assume charge of field operations. His choice was Colonel Robert E. Lee of the United States First Cavalry Regiment. Lee would later leave the American Army, declaring his loyalty to the Confederacy.

Grant's remark illustrates a deep fault line in the military, and one often blandly ignored—the fact that the officers who went with the South represented the cream of the crop. At the start of 1863, the influential *Harper's Weekly*, in an editorial titled "Have We a General Among Us?" began by admitting that of the seven men considered to be the best senior officers in the army, the best (Lee and Johnston) declared for the South and the two who remained loyal (Winfield Scott and Robert Patterson) were too old: "We have some thirty-eight to forty Major-Generals, and nearly three hundred Brigadiers; and now the question is, have we one man who can fairly be called a first-class General in the proper meaning of the term?"[4]

┼━━━┼

At the start of the war, Grant's (and Buell's) main opponent, Albert Sidney Johnston, was reckoned one of the most able officers in the country. Faced with such a formidable adversary, Buell fell prey to all sorts of wild imaginings, just as other Union generals would when facing Lee.

Grant simply couldn't fathom Buell's fear. It was, like his instinctive trust in his fellow man, a peculiar character flaw. He assumed that if he went to Nashville and conferred with Buell, his old classmate would quickly grasp the situation and react accordingly. The Confederates were forty or fifty miles away, and moving south. The thing to do was to move south after them.

Moreover, Grant, who had always ignored military protocol insofar as he was able, totally failed to understand that his presence put Buell in an awkward position. One of the problems that the Lincoln administration had never resolved was the question of the chain of command among those men holding the rank of Brigadier General or higher. Although Buell was still only a brigadier general and Grant was now a major general, Buell had a separate command, the Department of the Ohio, the troops in that department constituting the Army of the Ohio. So Buell's was the commander of a separate department, putting him on the same level as Halleck, who was also a departmental commander (the Department of the Missouri until March 8, 1862, and then the Department of the Mississippi). Buell, understandably, took the position that he was not subordinate to Grant, but reported directly to the overall army commander in Washington. The complication there was that in early March Lincoln had sacked George McClellan, who had replaced Winfield Scott as the nation's top military officer in November, 1861, and assumed the role of army commander himself. As Lincoln had no military experience and no military advisers, what this assumption meant in practice was that there was no one really in charge of the army.

From a military standpoint, Grant understood how urgent the matter was, which was why he went to Buell and tried to persuade him to move. But the meeting achieved nothing. Buell was not going to move south. Reason, strategy, and intelligence about Johnston had nothing to do with it. What the meeting did accomplish was to give Halleck an opportunity to claim that Grant was insubordinate. He had already been insinuating that Grant's men were thoroughly demoralized by the February campaign against the forts, that Grant had completely lost control of his command. Halleck had also hinted darkly that Grant had reverted to his old habits, presumably drunkenness.

In other words, Halleck was determined to get rid of Grant. He wrote to McClellan (who was still in supreme command of the armies), and asked to have Grant relieved of his command. His complaints were so vigorous that McClellan authorized Halleck to have Grant arrested and replaced with Charles F. Smith.

Halleck then informed Grant that he had been removed from his command, phrasing his message in such a way that Grant, who was entirely innocent of any wrongdoing whatsoever, asked Halleck to be relieved of all duties in his command.

But Halleck had overshot his mark. Back in Washington, Elihu Washburne, the Republican member of Congress from Galena who had been boosting the career of his fellow townsman from April 1861, got wind of what Halleck was doing and moved into action. Halleck suddenly found himself faced with potentially embarrassing questions from Washington regarding his complaints.

With McClellan gone, Halleck had little trouble getting the War Department to accede to what he had been after for months. So on March 11, 1862, the War Department consolidated the now obviously misnamed departments of Missouri and Ohio into one command under Halleck, who told Washington that he intended to take the field, and assume personal command of the two field armies, now concentrating along the Tennessee River close to the Mississippi state line.

Technically, the force Grant commanded was the Army of the District of Western Tennessee.[5] In an artfully sly response to the pressure coming from Washington thanks to Washburne's prodding of the War Department, Halleck now renamed that force. It was now to be called the Army of the Tennessee, and would be commanded by Grant, and Halleck claimed that the whole uproar about how Grant had allegedly been insubordinate was simply a misunderstanding.

Grant was not the only talented Union commander to have problems of this sort. Surprisingly few Union generals were spared. There was even a vicious campaign aimed at McClellan, who, it was alleged, was unstable to the point of being mentally ill.[6] The rumors and innuendo cost the Union dearly. On the one hand, it raised questions about Grant that never really went away. What was probably worse, however, was that this political maneuvering cost the Union precious time. Although Halleck had proposed that he would concentrate his forces for the drive south in March, three weeks later Buell's Army of the Ohio still hadn't joined up with the position occupied by the Army of the Tennessee, commanded by Grant. Grant had no option but to remain where he was.

Grant was deeply depressed. Alone among Union army commanders, he understood that with each passing week the South grew stronger, and that the war would thus be prolonged. But there was nothing he could do.

Halleck had ordered him to stay put until the Army of the Ohio joined up with his forces, at which point Halleck would personally take the field and direct a great offensive into Mississippi.

All Halleck would allow Grant to do was to move his forces further south, from the junction of the Tennessee and the Cumberland rivers with the Ohio. This was allowed only because Brigadier General William T. Sherman, who Grant had sent ahead of him to reconnoiter, discovered that the Confederates had abandoned all of the central portion of Tennessee. In other words, Grant had been right. Halleck allowed him to move the Army of the Tennessee down the river just upstream from Savannah, the location being chosen because the Army of the Ohio could join up with Grant's forces there.

Grant hadn't been able to get Buell to move because of Buell's exaggerated fears that Albert Sidney Johnston's enormous army would crush him. At the end of February 1862, that army did not exist. But now, as March turned to April, Johnston had brought that army into being. He had nearly 50,000 men gathering around Corinth, Mississippi, and now he made a momentous decision: to attack Grant's army and destroy it before Buell's forces could reach him. Faced with such a defeat, Buell would either retreat or dig in.

Either decision would be disastrous for the North. Whatever his reasons, whatever his motivation, Halleck had now given the upper hand and the initiative totally to Johnston.

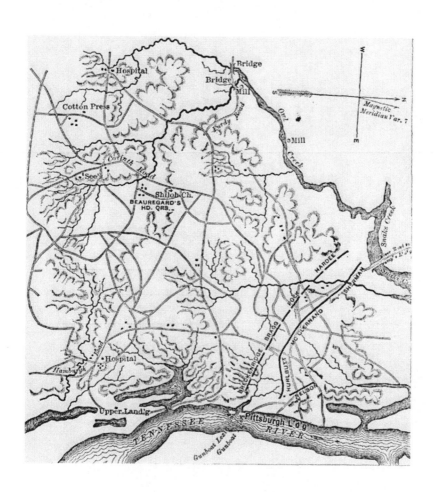

CHAPTER 6

Shiloh

Waterloo on the Tennessee

GRANT'S ARMY OF THE TENNESSEE WAS NOW CAMPED out just north of Savannah, Tennessee, along the Tennessee River, the troops strung out between two landings: Crump's and Pittsburg. Pittsburg Landing was the main northeasterly access route to Corinth, twenty-two miles distant. William Tecumseh Sherman, the brigadier general commanding the Fifth Infantry Division, had explored the ground along the river and found that the Confederate batteries there had long since been abandoned.

On March 19, 1862, Sherman sent Grant the following description: "am strongly impressed with the importance of this position, both for its defense by a small command, and yet affords admirable camping-ground for a hundred thousand men."[1]

Sherman was exactly right. The position was ideal for a defense: it would be difficult to mount penetrating offensive operations there. Although the road that led from the landing to Corinth was in decent shape, the land on either side was swampy and irregular, making it hard for advancing forces to spread out as they moved to the attack. Even if Johnston had the enormous army Buell believed he did, he would have difficulty bringing it to bear.

Both Grant and Johnston were supremely well-read men. It would scarcely have escaped either one of them that the situation was almost precisely like Waterloo in June 1815. Johnston's problem was exactly the same as the French emperor's: Napoleon had to beat Wellington before the Prussian Army joined with the British and their allies, at which point Napoleon would be outnumbered two to one.

The trick for Johnston was to time the attack so that the reinforcements would reach the scene too late. But if he attacked too early, the reinforcements could maneuver around him, striking his rear. But his strategy had one, larger weakness. Johnston knew that he, like Napoleon, would have to win decisively before Grant's reinforcements arrived. That gave Grant an advantage: like Wellington, he had only to hold his position until his reinforcements arrived. As the battle raged, the attackers would get weaker, and the defenders knew that their forces would become more powerful.

Now that the basic dilemma on each side is clear, the actual sequence of events becomes important. At Waterloo, the final act was late in the afternoon, when Napoleon threw in his elite force, the Imperial Guard, in one last, desperate attempt to break the Allied line. When that attack failed, the battle was lost, because the advance units of the Prussian Army were already deploying.

Shiloh conforms to this model with surprising fidelity. At 6:30 A.M., Johnston's forces attacked all along the three-mile front held by Grant's five divisions, forcing them back the length of the line. Brigadier General William Prentiss's Sixth Division of the Army of the Tennessee, in the center of the line, was the hardest hit: repeated blows from Braxton Bragg's Confederate Second Corps caused the men to quickly disperse.

But by midday, Sherman and Major General John McClernand, who commanded the divisions on Prentiss's flanks, counterattacked. They temporarily stopped the Confederate forward movement and even drove them back. For Johnston the problem was now maddeningly simple, at least in theory. His first aim had been to force his opponents back into the river, to hit them so hard that they would turn tail and run away. That hadn't happened, so now the key to a quick and decisive victory was to roll up the left flank of the Army of the Tennessee, separating the troops from the river itself, cutting them off from reinforcements and driving them downstream.

Tactically, given the terrain, Grant's right flank would have been preferable, but the right flank was the one that Major General Lew Wallace's Second Division of the Army of the Tennessee was slowly reinforcing. So Johnston threw everything he had into attacks against the left flank. But to no avail, and at around two o'clock, the Confederate commander, trying to rally his men for another attack, was mortally wounded and died from loss of blood. Shortly before three that bloody afternoon, Colonel Thomas Jordan, General G. T. Beauregard's adjutant, apparently turned to Beauregard, who, as second in command to Johnston, was now having to direct the battle. Jordan now elaborated one of the more striking figures of speech ever uttered by a man in the heat of battle:

> General, do you not think our troops are very much in the condition of a lump of sugar thoroughly soaked in water, but yet preserving its original shape though ready to dissolve? Would it not be judicious to get away with that we have?[2]

Beauregard, who had just assumed the command, agreed, and said that he was going to withdraw in a few minutes. Beauregard knew the story of Waterloo as well as any man alive, and knew that Johnston's gamble had failed. He was not, however, able to implement his intentions with much promptitude. Bragg, who had assumed command of the attack on the

Union left flank after Johnston's death, kept on fighting. He ordered four successive attacks, and it was this last, at nearly five in the afternoon, that resulted in the capture of the wounded General Prentiss, while the mortally wounded William Wallace, technically a Confederate prisoner, was left on the field.

+≻━◆━≺+

It was now about six in the evening, and Confederate commanders simply could not get their men to mount additional attacks on the Union defenses. They were exhausted, and too many of them had been killed or wounded—or had run away. Despite their best efforts, they had been unable to turn the flanks and pry Grant's army away from the river.

And at almost precisely the moment at which the final attacks were failing, Grant was receiving fresh troops. It is true that Johnston's reserves, Major General J. C. Breckinridge's Reserve Corps, were still largely untouched; but Breckinridge's command, although called a corps, was actually only the size of one of the Union divisions. So by dark, Grant had twice as many new troops deployed as the Army of Mississippi could manage.

More Union soldiers were yet to come. Nelson's troops were truly the advance guard of the Army of the Ohio. Brigadier General Thomas Crittenden's Fifth Division crossed the river during the night and was behind Nelson. One brigade of Brigadier General Alexander McCook's Second Division crossed the river early Monday morning and promptly went into action. The odds were changing rapidly in Grant's favor, and Monday would only see them lengthen, with the arrival of the rest of McCook's Second Division and Brigadier General Thomas Wood's Sixth Division. So by eight the next morning, Grant would have no less than three fresh divisions to deploy. Johnston's gamble had failed.

Consequently, Grant moved to the attack, steadily pushing in both of Beauregard's flanks. This basic idea about how to fight battles became the gold standard of the German army in both world wars: having repelled the enemy's attack, the army then would go on the offensive and would be left in possession of the battlefield. In 1944 the allies used the same principle against their German adversaries. They hung on at Normandy, and then, as the Germans became exhausted through attempts at containment, they broke through the German positions, and the breakthrough became a rout, with the German army streaming back into the Netherlands and Alsace, and abandoning France entirely. The principle Grant hit on at Shiloh would prove a durable one for the armies of the future.

+⊨═►═⊨+

All of us have a romantic mental image of great generals riding out in front of their troops and inspiring them to victory, something along the lines of the Jacques-Louis David's famous portrait of Napoleon on his great white charger, red cape billowing in the wind, right hand imperiously pointing forward. Given the extremely limited range and horrible inaccuracy of the smoothbore muskets of his opponents, such gestures were quite possible, and not all that risky. Of course as the forces deployed swelled from twenty or thirty thousand to a hundred thousand and more, it is doubtful that this sort of behavior really occurred. To a great extent this painterly image continues to dominate our imagination, but what we overlook is that the rifled musket made such gestures not only impractical, but suicidal. A general's duty, then, was not to lead from the front, but from the rear, and above all, not to get himself killed in action, for when he died, his plans died with him. "In war, men are nothing; one man is everything," is how Napoleon put it.[3]

As the German staff system slowly changed the basics of command and control of armies, this maxim became less and less true. Today it is hardly true at all. Commanding generals simply do not take charge on the battlefield, as much as they would like to do so. But the opposite was very much the case for the Civil War. Grant's behavior on that Sunday makes clear both what a successful commander had to do and how important he was.

J. F. C. Fuller is arguably Great Britain's most famous military historian. His masterful account of the battle of Shiloh is still the best one to date. Fuller lists eighteen separate items that Grant saw to, and his list may hardly be improved on. However, it may be easily divided into a few categories, and this enables us to see how Grant controlled the course of the battle.

Grant had already seen that on the battlefield the demand for ammunition was prodigious, so almost his first act after stepping off the boat in Savannah was to order more ammunition be sent forward. During the first day, he returned to this basic need, making sure that the soldiers holding the line didn't run out of ammunition. Logistics are never very glamorous, and in modern armies it is simply assumed that steady and serious efforts will be made to supply combat troops with ammunition and supplies. But in the Union army's organizational charts of 1862, no one was really responsible for such mundane affairs as making sure the men on the firing line had plenty of ammunition. No one had foreseen the prodigious expenditures of bullets that would mark every Civil War battle. It was assumed that soldiers would fire off the rounds they carried with them, and that by that point the battle would be over.

Having dealt with the ammunition problem, Grant now began to direct reinforcements. Although Prentiss's Sixth Division was in place on the battlefield, only seven of its infantry regiments were actually in position. Three of them (the fifteenth and sixteenth Iowa and the twenty-third Missouri) were still disembarking from the river on that morning. Grant immediately sent the Missouri regiment to reinforce Prentiss, and the two Iowa regiments to reinforce McClernand, directing them to form a skirmish line as they moved out, blocking the stragglers who were fleeing the battlefield and organizing them into units.

After logistics, reinforcements were key to winning the battle. As with Wellington at Waterloo, and Montgomery and Eisenhower at Normandy, Grant kept feeding troops into the line to stop the repeated Confederate attacks. At the same time he was deploying the three regiments, he directed Lew Wallace's Second Division, located downstream at Crump's Landing, to move to the battlefield.

In the days before radio and telephone communications, it was a truism among continental army commanders that when they heard gunfire somewhere, they marched toward the sound of the guns. Grant knew however that in his army this could not be assumed: troops had to be ordered up, and given injunctions to move. Wallace, for reasons best known to himself, managed to wander around north of the battle the entire day, which suggests that had he not been given a direct order and specific directions, his division would have never gotten to Shiloh at all. Almost simultaneously Grant directed Nelson, commanding the lead division of the Army of the Ohio, to move to the battle with all possible speed.

Neither general was able to make anything close to satisfactory progress: Wallace for some reason took the wrong road, and Nelson was tardy in ordering the move. Thus the two divisions that should have been on the battlefield by early afternoon—clearly a key point in the battle—didn't reach it until the evening, as we have seen. Realizing this, Grant sent for General Wood, directing him to move directly to Savannah, where his Sixth Division would find transport to cross the river, presumably thus able to threaten Johnston's right flank.

Clearly, his beleaguered troops were going to have to bear the brunt of the fighting without those three divisions, so as the battle raged, Grant began shifting regiments from the northern side of his line south to where the main Confederate effort was developing.

Napoleon had observed that the most important characteristic of a great commander is calm, a principle that is as true today as in his time. But this tranquility must be accurately transmitted to his subordinate commanders, so that it is not mistaken for denial, inertia, or incomprehension. Over the course of the war, Grant's behavior during battles became legendary. Under fire he exhibited a calm that was almost frightening to his subordinates: he would sit on a stump writing orders while shells exploded and cannon balls sailed by all around. By visiting each commander, he transmitted a calm assurance that victory would be theirs.

All of these activities involved movement, and during the course of this day Grant personally rode to where his divisional commanders were; he had conferred with each one before noon (and probably earlier). His calmness was accompanied by a realistic appreciation of the course of the battle. Sherman he visited twice, and it was on the second occasion, in the middle of the afternoon, that he told Sherman to be ready to attack the next day. In fights such as these, Grant observed, both sides felt themselves to be losing, so the one that went over to the attack was sure to win—yet another practical application of that early epiphany regarding fear. As we have seen, at almost that precise moment, Colonel Jordan was urging Beauregard to withdraw, and Beauregard agreed to do so.

There is also, Napoleon felt, the necessity for an instinct as to how things will play out. Great generals have the knack of being at the right place at the right time. By late afternoon, perceiving that the heaviest Confederate attacks would be on his left flank, Grant was there, and directed the first troops of Buell's army into position.

Grant's orders to Wood to move directly to Savannah suggest that he had a basic plan on how to fight the battle, should one develop, and this is reinforced by one of his final actions that evening, when he wrote out orders directing his divisions to advance the next morning, deployed so as to be ready to engage the enemy.

By contrast, Don Carlos Buell, Halleck's chief rival, was totally paralyzed. His main concern during the battle, insofar as it has been revealed to us, was an obsession regarding the thousands of stragglers who had fled the firing line for the safety of the bluffs along the river. His only real act was to threaten these poor fellows in an attempt to force them back into the battle, even though they were at that point little more than a disorganized mob.

Grant's realistic assessment of the flow of the battle and how to influence it was prescient. We can see echoes of that skill in the way that German officers in May 1940 intuited the course of the battle raging along the Meuse River and moved accordingly, thus inducing a state of panic in the French government that led directly to the allied collapse. Or, to use a more recent example, the sudden incursion into Baghdad by American forces in the Second Iraq War, which sent out an equally powerful signal.

When the final charges of the Old Guard had failed him at Waterloo, Napoleon fled the field, and his army had simply dissolved, just as the Army of the Potomac had collapsed at First Bull Run. In the two world wars, such collapses rarely happened, as modern armies had a much denser network of officers in place to make sure that the withdrawal, however rapid it might be, was controlled.

In this sense Shiloh was the first of the great modern battles, and not like Waterloo at all. Although Beauregard was subsequently tagged the "Napoleon in Gray," at Shiloh he proved himself made of sterner stuff. As Grant's divisions advanced the next morning, they ran into stiff opposition. The fighting on the second day of Shiloh was nothing like that of the first day, but it established quickly enough that the Army of Mississippi, although beaten, was far from whipped. There was no panic-stricken flight of a beaten army; instead, there was a well-managed retreat of the sort that one usually associates only with trained professionals, the kind of systematic retreat that marked the German evacuation of Sicily in the Second World War.

This degree of professionalism, as exhibited by the discipline of both Union and Confederate officers and men, is a striking fact about the fight at Pittsburg Landing. Instead of launching one attack and then quitting the fight, Johnston's Southerners attacked again and again. So too with the Army of the Tennessee: instead of engaging in one defensive action and then fleeing the field after the first bloodletting, Grant's soldiers not only kept on fighting, but launched repeated counterattacks throughout that first day.

In terms of numbers, Shiloh was the first great engagement of the war, and both sides were shaken by the casualties. Confederate losses were easily one in four, while Grant's losses were about one in five. Although one must be wary of false precision in these figures, the number of men killed in action was about the same for both sides: 1,784 Union soldiers and 1,723 Confederates. The same data gives fairly close figures for the wounded: 8,408 Union and 8,012 Confederates.[4] Although even more devastating battles would follow, Shiloh is still the ninth bloodiest battle of the Civil War.

This in turn would give rise to the charge that Grant won because he simply overpowered his adversaries, that he was, basically, a butcher. This claim, fanned by professional rivalries and hysterical newspaper reporters, was largely a result of American provincialism. Casualties at Shiloh were lower than those sustained during numerous Napoleonic battles, Waterloo and Borodino being only the most famous. But for a North accustomed to being told tall tales of bloodless Union victories (few of which actually occurred), the intensity of the struggle fell on an astonished public like a thunderbolt.

Shiloh was certainly a desperate battle. The intensity can be measured by the loss in senior officers. Of the roughly eighty Union regimental, brigade, and division commanders, forty-five were casualties by the end of the battle. The same can be said for the Confederates, who lost two corps commanders (out of four), three division commanders (out of five), and four brigade commanders (out of sixteen).

The heavy toll taken of these, the most senior officers, would hit the Confederacy particularly hard, although it was rightly eclipsed by the death of Albert Sidney Johnston.

Before the war Johnston had been justly hailed as one of the nation's best generals. His influence on the Confederate leadership was considerable, and it is tempting to consider how the war would have played out had he been alive to make the case for how the Confederacy could win. Although Grant ruined his defensive strategy in February 1862, and then destroyed his army at Shiloh, Johnston's reputation was deserved: he just happened to be the first general to go down in defeat when he encountered Grant. He would not be the last.

The ferocity of the fighting and the level of loss at Shiloh led Grant to what may fairly be termed the conceptual breakthrough he mentions rather casually in his memoirs:

> Up until the battle of Shiloh, I, as well as thousands of other citizens, believed that the rebellion against the Government would collapse suddenly and soon, if a decisive victory could be gained over any of its armies. . . . But when Confederate armies were collected which not only attempted to hold a line . . . but assumed the offensive and made such a gallant effort to regain what had been lost, then, indeed, I gave up all idea of saving the Union except by complete conquest.[5]

Nothing made this clearer than Beauregard's handling of the retreating forces. Shiloh was a defeat, not a rout. Although no one in the North realized it yet, the implications of Shiloh are tragically clear in retrospect: it was going to be a long, hard, war.

Although we usually see the Civil War as a titanic struggle to the death, a war that would only end with the complete destruction of one side or the other, very few people on either side envisioned it this way in April 1861. Interestingly enough, a year later there was still a widespread feeling in the North that after a few reverses, the South would quit.

When Sherman, echoing the dour predictions of the aging Winfield Scott, had observed that it would take nearly a quarter of a million men to seize the offensive in Mississippi, he had been ridiculed as a madman. And for the first year of the war, it was easy to construe—or to willfully misinterpret—what was happening as proof that the two men were flat out wrong, and that the Halleckites were on the right track, that the rebellion could be outmaneuvered with very little actual fighting.

At a time when this idea was still ascendant, Grant began to see the truth. The war was going to go on for years, it would be a bloody affair, and if the Union persisted in its misguided strategies on how to fight it, the Confederacy could very well win. Grant was confident that the Union could prevail, but so far, he had seen no evidence to that effect.

By the same reckoning, however, Shiloh reinforced his idea that the Union would prevail. The Confederacy had been much quicker off the mark in organizing its forces, its technical decisions on organization had given it another great advantage, and the men given the senior commands were enormously more competent than their Northern counterparts. In many ways, Shiloh can be seen as the greatest blow the South could deliver.

However, despite the valor and military competence of the Confederates, Shiloh was a great Union victory in every sense. The outcome was clear and indisputable: the Army of Mississippi had attacked, and been forced to retreat, leaving the armies of Tennessee and Ohio in possession of the field of battle, and on the brink of seizing the important rail junction at Corinth, as well as most of the northern portion of the state of Mississippi, an important bridgehead from which to launch attacks into the heart of the Confederacy.

Nor were the results of the battle inconclusive. Johnston had sought to destroy the Army of the Tennessee before it could be reinforced by the

Army of the Ohio, and failed in his aim. It could hardly be claimed that the battle was indecisive, or that Beauregard's actions had been some sort of strategic withdrawal. Although he may have been exaggerating, the new Confederate commander's assertion that at nightfall he had barely twenty thousand men in the field is certainly credible.

Although it's easy to drift into pure speculation, it's certainly not speculation that the other Union commanders would have quit the battle. Charles Smith, the most experienced and respected of the generals, the man Halleck had put in command when he had been trying to get rid of Grant in early March, had been forced to relinquish command and leave the army owing to ill health. That left Buell, Sherman, and McClernand, as William Wallace lay dying on the battlefield and Prentiss, also wounded, had been taken prisoner.

Of course retrospectively, everyone was full of fight, but on Sunday evening it was a far different story. Buell, for example, clearly wanted to retreat. Sherman, despite his ingenuous assertion that his men were in "good spirits" and were determined to "redeem" the day's losses, clearly assumed they would withdraw.

Buell—and every other Union commander—would have thus given the Confederacy a victory of enormous proportions, one far greater than Bull Run. So although Johnston's decision was a desperate gamble, had anyone else been in command it might well have succeeded. Johnston failed, first because of Grant's management of the defense on the first day, and second because of Grant's unshakable determination on Sunday evening to begin the next morning with a massive offensive that would drive the Army of Mississippi entirely off the field.

Although the North was certainly willing to accept Shiloh for the great victory that it was, and although Grant was briefly the man of the hour, the curious fact about the aftermath of the victory is that it crystallized the extremely negative portrayal of Grant that began to emerge. It would have a lasting effect on his reputation, and would never quite go away.

1. Grant on a plinth at Vicksburg. The face, obscured from any point of view, inadvertently symbolizes the opinions of his biographers. (John Mosier)

2. *Grant in the field. In appearance, the most unmilitary of generals. (National Archives)*

3. *Grant with his staff. They all look more like victorious generals than their chief. Notice the characteristic slouch. (National Archives)*

4. *Grant in 1865. The only portrait of him that comes close to capturing the man himself. (National Archives)*

5. Sketch of Grant's head. The lack of detail allows a glimpse into his character. (National Archives)

6. *Parrott 20-pounder. Rifled guns such as this American design made fortifications built before 1860 obsolete. (John Mosier)*

7. *The Bend of the Mississippi as seen from the gun batteries at Vicksburg. (John Mosier)*

8. *A road in Mississippi, looking much like it did in 1863. The reason for the importance of railroads and rivers. (John Mosier)*

9. *Grant's hastily assembled artillery, like this 12-pounder seen on the Vicksburg battlefield, persuaded the Confederates to surrender rather than withstanding a prolonged siege.*

10. The new lieutenant general: Grant in 1864

11. The commander of all the Union armies: Grant in March 1865.

CHAPTER 7

Aftermath

Blaming the Victor

GRANT HAD NOW DIRECTED THE ONLY TWO MAJOR Union victories in a year of warfare. One might assume this would have brought about a sea change in the perception of the war, with everyone from Lincoln to the man in the street acknowledging two painfully obvious facts: it was going to be a long and bloody struggle, and Grant was the only man who could win and thus end it. Alas for the nation, as well as for its best general, this shift in perception did not occur.

In the aftermath of Shiloh, professional jealousies and wildly irresponsible journalists contrived to effect exactly the opposite perception. In January 1863, in an editorial cited earlier titled "Have We a General Among

Us?" the editors of *Harper's Weekly* dismissed Grant with a few sentences. He was "very fortunate" at Donelson, and was nearly "destroyed at Shiloh," saved only "by accidents beyond his control."[1]

There were five reasons why this negative opinion of Grant not only persisted but was exacerbated by Shiloh: the level of casualties; the need to find a scapegoat for Northern failures; the reportage of an irresponsible and inexperienced press; fundamental misunderstandings about the battle; and the behavior of Halleck. Taken together, they were sufficient to cloud Grant's reputation. Essentially, his treatment after Shiloh was simply a repetition of his treatment after Donelson. It was not until July 1863, when he captured Vicksburg, that public opinion began to turn. When it turned, it turned quickly, but from April 1862 to October 1863, when he was placed in command of the western theater, Grant was almost universally disparaged and abused. He had spent a long time in the wilderness of public opinion before he ever saw the actual wilderness of northern Virginia.

In spring 1862, Northern journalists and their readers were still envisioning the rebellion as being a replay of the Mexican War, when a small force of Americans had achieved a very great victory at a very small cost in human life. Not only was victory assumed, but it was a victory on the cheap, a notion pandered to by some of the Union's generals, with their intellectualization of warfare. The casualty rate at Shiloh shattered all of these assumptions. Those losses may have been consistent with losses in other great battles, and they would soon be surpassed by other struggles, but in May 1862 they were sharply at odds with the general perceptions.

In the global context, the Civil War was not a uniquely bloody struggle. But for the vast majority of Americans, unfamiliar with the carnage of the Napoleonic battlefields, Shiloh was a traumatic event.

This leads to a point about the losses that is qualitative rather than quantitative. The armies of the Napoleonic wars, like those fighting the surprisingly savage battles of the eighteenth century, were mostly composed of soldiers taken from the dregs of society, with the preferred method of recruiting often looking suspiciously like kidnapping. Basically, society didn't care whether these men lived or died, and in the end viewed their deaths and suffering with indifference.

By contrast, the men who suffered at Shiloh represented a cross section of American society, as did the Prussians of 1870. Although it is well known that conscription was abused, and particularly in the Union, by definition the idea of universal military service means that males from almost every segment of society will be in uniform. The loss of these men sent shock waves through society at a level that had not been seen before, and in this one sense the Civil War was truly the first modern war.

This perception explains why increasingly in modern society, losses that in previous centuries were accepted with equanimity are now seen as socially disastrous. The men who die in battle are much more an integral part of society than had historically been the case. This also means that the population at large, regardless of race or class, is more directly affected by these losses and as a consequence is more likely to question the reasons behind the war, as in the case of Vietnam and the current war in Iraq. But there's more—as soldiers become specialists, the loss of each individual has a greater impact on the war itself, the death of a common soldier today creates a situation analogous to the death of a commander in the past

In this respect Grant was very much a modern general: he was deeply pained by casualties, and regretted having to order operations that he knew would result in great losses. Nor did he attempt to insulate himself from the men he was ordering into battle. Like the French general Phillipe Pétain in 1916, and Dwight D. Eisenhower in 1944, he moved among them, giving them the one great gift of which he was capable: confidence that they would prevail.

From this trauma, which was new and horrific for American society and the world, Grant had drawn a disturbing and prescient conclusion: if the Confederates could fight like this, it was going to be a long and costly war. But that required an admission: that the other side was militarily competent. Although this recognition was slowly dawning inside the Union army, the population at large continued to labor under the impression that all that was required to disperse the rebellion was a good swift kick.

In other words, the complacency of the population, fed by the government and the press, when confronted with the level of loss at Shiloh, responded with an understandable reflex. There was a growing feeling in the nation that the reason that swift blow hadn't been administered thus far was simple: incompetence. The casualties at Shiloh seemed simply the bloody confirmation of this.

The assumption was not all that far off. Where it was wrong was when it came to particular cases. Sherman was not insane, McClellan was not mentally ill, Grant was not an incompetent drunk. However, given the persistence of the Northern mindset about a cheap and easy war, the only conceivable explanation for the difficulties of the struggling Union armies was managerial ineptitude. Given the senior Union generals, this was certainly a reasonable assumption; in this case it happened to be wrong, but people simply hadn't yet begun to accept the fact that the South was not only determined to fight, but militarily capable of doing so.

Not that Southerners felt any differently. Both sides entered the war with a sublime contempt for their enemy's military prowess, and viewed the setbacks their side endured as proof not of the valor and skill of their opponent, but in terms of errors made by their own leaders.

✦━━✦

But in the North this combination of complacency, denial, and outrage had a public voice: the newspapers, and sensationalistic accounts of Shiloh by naïve and often unscrupulous reporters fueled the growing sense of Northern outrage over why the Union had not yet prevailed.[2] In this sense the Civil War is curiously contemporary. In the world wars (and in Korea), journalists were heavily controlled. Their movements were restricted, and what they were allowed to write was censored. When they were allowed access to operations, in the modern parlance "embedded" in combat units, their reports were retrospective and controlled. But in the Civil War, Union journalists wandered about freely, reported whatever they liked, and saw as much as they dared, in terms of combat.

Despite the emphasis on individual rights (as long as the subject was restricted to institutions controlled by white males), the Confederate government exerted a remarkable control over the press. It did not approach the control that the British and French had after September 1914, when journalists were not only censored, but not even allowed anywhere near combat troops and the front lines, but in contrast with the Union, the press was tightly controlled. On the other side, Northern journalists enjoyed a freedom of the press that was well nigh absolute.

Not surprisingly—and this too is a parallel with the present day—most of what journalists saw they were unable to interpret correctly.[3] Nor was there any serious attempt to understand what was happening: everything was subordinated to sensationalism and melodrama.

So this freedom was grossly abused. Grant records reading in the papers an almost verbatim account of an instruction given to one of his staff officers; one reporter was caught eavesdropping on a briefing he was giving to his commanders.[4] Over the course of the war, Northern reporters fabricated stories, reported military plans, divulged troop movements, and provided the Confederates with a consistent stream of vital military intelligence. In so doing they inaugurated an adversarial relationship that has endured to this day, and one that transcends national boundaries.

How this related to Shiloh and Grant is simple enough. From the safety of the river, the journalists reporting on Shiloh saw a disheartening sight: thousands of terrified men who had fled the battlefield that morning, either on their own or because their equally terrified officers had fled to the rear as well. There is no doubting either the numbers or the terror. Nor is there any doubting that this phenomenon was hardly restricted to raw recruits from North America. Wellington's comment on this phenomenon is not nearly as well known as it should be: "They all do it at some time or other"; like Grant, he clearly didn't mind, as long as they subsequently returned to service.[5]

We often attribute such behavior to cowardice, to thinking that it is the logical result of the horrors of war, or in thinking that it was totally a function of the lack of professionalism in the armies themselves. These Union soldiers were mostly raw recruits who had never seen combat, civilians in uniform without the extensive military training that would ensure such things didn't happen on the battlefield. However, this fear and lack of professional training is not necessarily a determining factor in judging an army. When the distinguished French historian and combat veteran Jean-Norton Cru wrote his seminal study of war narratives, in his chapter on false ideas about war, one of the first false ideas he listed were the twin notions of "courage and fear: good soldiers are brave, bad soldiers afraid."[6]

As the nineteenth century wore on, professional staffs in Europe began to employ military police specifically for the purpose of preventing flight and rounding up stragglers. All armies had such units. But it was not until 1915 that the British military police were specifically detailed to deal with what armies euphemistically call stragglers. Before then, the general idea was pretty much what Wellington had said and what Grant himself observed: they ran away but generally they all came back. Sweeping up stragglers and getting them back into the fight was incidental to winning the engagement.

But for inexperienced observers, whose first sight of the conflict was the mass of demoralized and frightened men, it seemed that all was lost, and that the main cause was the ineptitude of Army commanders. Bluntly, it was either that or admit, in the parlance of the day, that the Union Army was full of cowards. Or—more unthinkable still—that the Confederate forces were militarily competent.

The Northern journalists on the Tennessee had no one to guide them, and psychologically, what they saw was extremely difficult to square with notions of how great battles were fought, much less how victories were won. They had no concept of warfare, but they could certainly recognize panic and confusion when they saw it: "The distant rear of an army engaged in battle is not the best place from which to judge correctly what is going on at the front," is how Grant put it with his usual understated sarcasm.[7] The same holds true today, although one could argue that the front of an army often appears confused and chaotic as well—and is just as difficult to interpret.

Although sober and respectable journals like *Harper's* touted Pittsburg Landing as a substantial victory (which it was), with a full-page portrait gallery of "Our Heroes," hysterical and often wildly inaccurate accounts of the battle, as seen from the safety of the river, soon began to emerge.

In the short run, these wild accusations cast a considerable pall on Grant's competence, and they explain why the worth of the Union's only consistently victorious general didn't begin to be recognized until after the fall of Vicksburg in July 1863—and then only grudgingly. The legend of the drunken butcher was created at Shiloh by irresponsible journalists, carefully nurtured by jealous officers, and then given an unexpected lease on life by Southern apologists as they spun the conflict into the myths of the Lost Cause. The result has been to see Shiloh as a sort of victory *manqué*, just as the editors of *Harper's* did in January 1863.

The impression one came away with was that the Confederates had come close to winning a great victory, owing to Grant's carelessness or lack of proper military training: he was surprised; he did not expect a battle; his men weren't even entrenched. Shiloh was a Union victory, but only because Grant was able to improvise, recover from his initial errors—the errors of an amateur—and because the opposing general, Johnston, was killed in action.

The argument that Grant was taken by surprise is a red herring, and rests basically on confusion about what the word *surprise* means in the context of matters military. In June 1815, Wellington's dispatches to London assured the government that he had no anticipation that Napoleon would attack him. His response on learning that Napoleon was moving to attack him is an excellent summation of what Grant must have thought: "Humbugged, by God!"[8]

Grant certainly did not plan to fight a battle on the heights above Pittsburg Landing, but to claim that he was therefore surprised is disingenuous. He had made his own surprise attacks, but, given the situation in April 1862, he did not feel that the probability of an enemy attack was very high. On the other hand, like any great commander, he had prudently disposed of his forces so that they could deal with whatever developed. The key criterion here is disposition of force. Although Johnston, like Napoleon, hoped to achieve a victory by destroying one enemy army before the other could combine with it, in both cases their opponents (Grant and Wellington, respectively) had units positioned so as to enable them to fight the attackers to a draw.

As the course of the fighting has established, Grant's dispositions proved well suited for the battle. The right flank, for example, the one most susceptible to being turned, was the position closest to the position occupied by his reserve division encamped at Crump's Landing. Grant may have been humbugged, but, like Wellington, he was hardly caught off balance.

This attitude explains why both generals were candid in saying before the battle that they didn't expect there would be one. Much has been made of Grant's "carelessness" in not readying his forces for an attack, and even more is made of one of his exasperated responses to Halleck: "I have not the faintest apprehension of an attack." Interestingly, one can find the same bland assurances in Wellington's correspondence.[9]

Grant's confidence was not a result of deficiencies; rather it was a function of how he had disposed of his troops and the position they occupied. Curiously, critics of Grant have ignored this last point, despite its obvious importance. Instead, they have concentrated on the second supposed failure, the failure to have his men dig entrenchments. This idea is even more bogus than the notion of surprise, as it overlooks two basic facts.

The first of these is that Grant's engineering officer, James B. McPherson, had surveyed the land leading up to the bluffs and concluded that lines of entrenchments were not practicable given the gullies and ravines that ran roughly perpendicular to the river. The only two possibilities for workable trench lines were either too far out from or too close to the river.

The problem at Shiloh was that the only practicable defensive trench line was so close to the river that there wouldn't be any room for the defenders to reinforce the position if attacked. Crucial to any static defensive line was the need for territory behind the line that would enable units to be moved laterally to threatened points, and to mass for counterattacks.

The broken terrain, mostly covered with brush, combined with the roads and creeks, offered plenty of natural cover, particularly on the left flank:

Here behind a dense thicket on the crest of a hill was posted a strong force of as hardy troops as ever fought, almost perfectly protected by the conformation of the ground. To assail it an open field had to be passed. . . . No figure of speech would be too strong to express the deadly peril of an assault upon this natural fortress."[10]

It was, as this diehard partisan of the Confederacy observes elsewhere in his account, "impregnable." Grant's position, as seen from the Confederate side, did not seem nearly so carelessly chosen: this then was the second fact that is overlooked.

The battle of Shiloh was an absolutely decisive engagement: Johnston's aim was not to bloody the Union army, or to slow it down. It was to annihilate it completely, just as Napoleon aimed to do at Waterloo. Increasingly, there has been a tendency to assume that the Confederacy was doomed from the start. This is simply not the case. The claim that when Shiloh was lost, the cause was lost, is quite true.

Mostly owing to its importance, Shiloh is perhaps the engagement most dominated by what Grant derisively called "ifs."

> *Ifs* defeated the Confederates at Shiloh. There is little doubt that we would have been disgracefully beaten *if* all the shells and bullets fired by us had [flown] harmlessly over the enemy and *if* all theirs had taken effect. (*Memoirs*, 188–189)

This is a marvelous passage. The varying accounts and interpretations of Shiloh begin a long and confused history of *ifs*, in which the course of the war—and the abilities of its commanders—are endlessly spun and deconstructed. Shiloh is not important only because of its outcome; it is important because of the stories told about it.

Speculations are always fascinating, but we must consider every possible contingency when making them, not simply the one that suits a particular point of view. Speculations about Shiloh quickly founder, as there are as many "ifs" on Grant's side as there are on Johnston's. How would Shiloh have turned out if Wallace's troops had been in action on the right flank that morning? How would it have turned out had Nelson's division started out promptly, instead of dawdling until one in the afternoon? There are as many suppositions supporting a crushing Union victory as a Confederate one. We must therefore restrict ourselves to reasonable certainties.

Just as the Unionists couldn't bear to admit that the Confederates were fielding a tough and competent army, and thus had to see Shiloh as evidence of Grant's ineptitude, so on the Confederate side there had to be a scapegoat for why defeat was snatched from the jaws of victory. It was, William Preston Johnston opines, all on account of Beauregard, who decided to withdraw, when instead he should have pressed on.

The result is a curious sort of history. Shiloh was a Confederate defeat because of Beauregard's incompetence or timidity; it was nearly a Confederate victory because of Grant's carelessness. In this regard Shiloh sets the pattern for much that has been written about the war, which thus takes shape as an account of failures and contingencies, as a demonstration of bumbling, in which hundreds of thousands of Americans were slaughtered owing to fundamental errors made by the generals.

In reality—or as close to it as we are likely to get—Shiloh was a desperate struggle because it matched a military genius with an experienced and able general of the first rank, because their subordinates were first-class officers, and because the soldiers on both sides fought with exemplary courage.

CHAPTER 8

Victory Out of Despair

GRANT'S REWARD FOR SHILOH WAS TO BE REMOVED from command of the Army of the Tennessee. The official reason for this was that Halleck, who had arrived at Hamburg Landing, five miles above Pittsburg Landing, on April 11, 1862, had now concentrated his forces into one enormous army and was assuming direct command. There were now over 100,000 men concentrated around the battlefield: Buell's Army of the Ohio, Pope's Army of the Mississippi, and what had formerly been Grant's Army of the Tennessee. Halleck reorganized them into a textbook formation of left, center, right, and reserve, but broke up Grant's army and gave command of what was left of his forces to Major General George Thomas.

Grant records the reorganization in this fashion: "I was named second in command, and was also supposed to be in command of the right wing and reserve."[1] But this promotion was simply a bureaucratic dodge to remove Grant from effective command, Halleck having learned from his attempt in February that he couldn't fire Grant outright. The Union's most victorious general was, as Grant himself remarked, "little more than an observer" (*Memoirs*, 196). In reality, he was more of a prisoner, for all practical purposes under arrest. Halleck issued orders directly to the other commanders, completely ignoring Grant, except for ordering him to stay at headquarters.

If Grant's position was personally embarrassing, what he observed horrified him. By April 30, Halleck had assembled his enormous army and proceeded to advance on Corinth, twenty-odd miles to the south of Shiloh. It took him the better part of a month to move his army that far, and it was not until May 30 that he was ready to begin his siege. Halleck's rate of advance, twenty-two miles in thirty days, established a record of sorts, albeit not one that any general would wish to hold.

Grant, swallowing his pride, tried to give Halleck the benefit of his advice, as he saw clearly enough that the whole operation would end in a few days. But he was rebuffed, "I was silenced so quickly that I felt possibly I had suggested an unmilitary movement."[2] Grant understood more than the necessity for speed: he saw that Halleck was squandering the advantages that the Union had briefly enjoyed after Shiloh.[3]

What was gnawing at Grant was not just the injustice of his treatment, but the realization that Halleck was empowering the Union's adversaries. Now that Johnston's gamble at Shiloh had failed, the problem confronting the Confederacy in the Mississippi Valley was how to block the Union advance without risking its forces in another great battle. Inside the Confederacy, Shiloh was seen as a brilliant Confederate coup, and Grant's lateral move to a vague position under Halleck with no assigned duties—or troops to command—suggested to the Confederates that their adversaries in Mississippi had no stomach for combat.

As Grant was gloomily aware, Halleck's slow advance suggested to Beauregard, now commanding the Confederate forces in Mississippi, that he could simply outmaneuver the Union juggernaut. So his men remained tantalizingly out of reach, knowing that Halleck wouldn't close with them. Beauregard maneuvered slyly around Corinth, and then, at the last moment, simply abandoned the position and left his opponent standing there rather foolishly. When Union soldiers entered Corinth on May 30, 1862, they found a city that had been totally abandoned. There were hardly even any civilians left.

In Halleck's mind, he had won a great victory, and with hardly any fighting, thus confirming his view of himself as a Napoleon in blue. After all, Corinth was a strategic rail junction, vital to the Confederacy, and now he had seized it. Beauregard had been outmaneuvered, Halleck believed, and was afraid to give battle when confronted with a determined and judicious commander.

Grant however was in despair. He knew exactly what Beauregard was doing and why, and as he watched, Halleck made plans to fritter away his enormous army by sending units hither and yon in pursuit of tangential objectives, while the troops around Corinth fortified the town in such fashion that in Grant's estimate it would have taken 100,000 men to hold the defenses.

For Grant, the great lesson of Shiloh was that the Confederates were deadly serious about their rebellion, that they were not going to quit after a few reverses, that they really were determined to launch a successful state. Having realized this problem long before anyone else, Grant now pondered its implications, one reason he was so distressed at what he saw going on.

In addition to prolonging the war, Grant also saw the practical military problem that Halleck was creating. He was proceeding as though the Union was fighting two separate Confederacies, one in the east, one in the west, completely isolated from one another. But what Grant realized was that in fact the Confederacy was a surprisingly unified state, particularly when it came to military operations. Halleck's vast army should have been used in such a way that the Confederate high command would either have to move troops west in large numbers, or lose the Mississippi River Valley entirely.

But once the Confederates had figured out what Halleck was doing, they realized they could capitalize on it, and divert their resources to the east. The senior Confederate generals saw a golden opportunity of the sort Albert Sidney Johnston had seen: carry the war directly to the enemy, hit him so hard that he'll quit the war. In the east, which the Confederates saw—correctly—was the place to hit and ensure maximum panic, Robert E. Lee was winding up for his great sweep north.

Not only was the war going to continue, but the Union was actually inching closer to defeat. Grant's despair was not personal. Of course he took the criticisms and the treatment by Halleck personally, as any human being would. But his real despair was caused by the consequences for his country. Grant is often seen as a cipher, an enigma, but his motivations were quite simple. He was a good old-fashioned patriot, and what hurt his country injured him.

+━━◆━━+

In June, Grant was at the low point of his life, in such despair that he tried to resign. Of course this played directly into Halleck's hands. Halleck wrote a disingenuous letter in response to Grant's offer of resignation expressing bland surprise at how Grant could feel as he did. After all, he was second in command of what was the largest Union force in the field.

But owing to inadequate sanitation and a general ignorance about disease, this army was shrinking at an alarming rate, exposing yet another of the numerous flaws in Halleck's ideas about warfare. In terms of battlefield performance, both Union and Confederate troops were already demonstrating how good they were. Shiloh would have been a credit to any two European armies. Where they fell dismally short was in logistics and support services, and nowhere was this more apparent than in the basic arrangements necessary to support an army in the field. This had always been the case, but as field armies got bigger, so did the problem. Halleck could brag about taking Corinth with hardly any battlefield casualties, but by June 1, 1862, less than two-thirds of his force was able to fight, as more and more men fell sick. Grant, who had an iron constitution, was one of the few officers not debilitated by dysentery. Even Halleck suffered from this complaint.

Sanitation is always a problem in armies, and given the conditions in which most soldiers work, sickness is a serious problem. Competent medical services and an emphasis on cleanliness can remedy the problem, and in contemporary armies has done so. But a certain amount of this is simply inevitable in places where large numbers of soldiers are stationed on a temporary basis: the American army in the First World War and the Canadians in the Second World War both had serious problems in this regard. That is why contemporary armies devote so much attention to basics of preventive medicine, public health, and even simple sanitary arrangements, the result being that nowadays most soldiers are actually fit for duty, a striking contrast with previous conflicts.

As sickness decimated their ranks, morale sank. Like Buell, Halleck had no appreciation for the sort of army he was commanding. He behaved as though it was the army from a past age, composed of men from the bottom rung of society, men who could be whipped into line and turned into perfect peacetime soldiers, and, more importantly, men whose basic living arrangements could be completely ignored.

But once again, fate intervened. By July 1862, despite the inconvenience that wartime had posed to his career, Halleck had vanquished all his rivals very effectively. He was now poised to win the greatest victory of the war. In March, Lincoln had assumed the supreme command, but he quickly realized he needed some military officer in Washington he could rely on for advice. So on July 11, 1862, Halleck, the only senior general who, thanks to Grant, had some vague claim to success, was named commander in chief.

Halleck's lateral promotion of Grant now boomeranged: since he was supposedly second in command, he now assumed control over the army in the west, and Halleck couldn't do much about it. What he did do was to take as many troops away from Grant as possible, hoping to weaken his command to the point that he couldn't do anything but defend the territory that had been seized.

Lincoln, without realizing it, now came to Halleck's aid. The president wanted to win the war, but he had no real idea how to go about it, and as the clock ticked away, he drifted further and further away from the initial appreciations of Winfield Scott and John C. Frémont about the importance of the west. Unlike the politicians and rear-echelon experts in

Washington, Lincoln was concerned about more than the eastern seaboard, but his eye was fixed not on the river valley, but on strategically worthless east Tennessee.

Although American historians tend to give Lincoln the benefit of the doubt when it comes to military affairs, British military historians are blunt: "Once again, through sheer ignorance of strategy, had Lincoln missed an opportunity of shortening the war," is how one of them puts it; while another one opines that Eastern Tennessee "was a purely political objective with no military potential value. . . . . Owing to Lincoln's obsession with East Tennessee, the Mississippi Valley was for the time relegated to the status of a secondary theater, although that waterway offered the most direct approach to the heart of the Confederacy."[4]

Lincoln's obsession coincided neatly enough with Halleck's pretensions. So in early June, Buell was sent to occupy the area, and over the next three months, Halleck peeled off four divisions from Grant and sent them eastward. He had already dispersed the enormous army he had gathered around Corinth, but when Grant had assumed command, he had 64,000 men. Two months later Grant had a little over 40,000 and Buell had over 50,000.

The dispersal of force, together with the extreme slowness of Buell's advance, gave the new Confederate commander, Braxton Bragg, precisely the opportunity to strike that Grant had foreseen in June. Bragg had plenty of men now. By early October, Buell, Halleck, and Lincoln had lost all their earlier gains, and Union troops had been forced to fall back on Kentucky. To add insult to injury, General Kirby Smith now captured the state capital (Frankfort) and tried to move Kentucky into the Confederacy.

In the east, Lee began his great sweep into the Union, and the bill for Halleck's sloth and Lincoln's strategic mismanagement came due at the end of August. Second Bull Run was the perfect illustration of what the North had been resolutely ignoring. Lee was grossly outnumbered: he had barely 50,000 men and Pope had nearly 80,000.

Lee not only beat his enemy on the battlefield, but he won the casualty exchange as well. In his next battle, Antietam, he wasn't so fortunate. Although conventionally seen as a Union victory, September 17, 1862, was the single bloodiest day of the war, and McClellan was unable to transform his substantial manpower advantage (over two to one by most accounts) into a real victory. Grant saw this coming. As he described the situation:

> I was much concerned because my first duty, after holding the territory acquired within my command, was to prevent further reinforcing of Bragg in Middle Tennessee. Already the Army of Northern Virginia had defeated the army under General Pope and was invading Maryland. In the Center General Buell was on his way to Louisville and Bragg marching parallel to him with a large Confederate force for the Ohio River.[5]

The third prong of the Confederate offensive was aimed squarely at Grant, who had sensibly moved his headquarters to Jackson, Tennessee, where he could safeguard the extended lines of communication and move his meager reserves to counter the next Confederate moves. As Grant would reveal in his *Memoirs,* this was the most anxious period of the war: the south was everywhere on the offensive, he was outnumbered, and his forces were spread all over the region trying to fend off Confederate cavalry raids aimed at knocking out the rail lines.

The offensive was not long in coming, and began with a disaster. The Confederate Major General Sterling Price was ordered to take Corinth, and began by seizing Iuka, about twenty-five miles to the east along the rail line. The Union commander fled the town without firing a shot, and the town fell on September 14, leaving Price's men to outfit themselves with the massive supplies stored at the rail depot.

Price only had 14,000 men—not enough to take Corinth—so he had to wait for the arrival of Major General Earl van Dorn, commander of the Confederate Army of the West. What followed was a race. Grant's plan was to bring Price to battle before van Dorn could reach him, and to this end he sent Major General William Ord, one of his best commanders, down the rail line with about 8,000 men, while Brigadier General

William Rosecrans, with a slightly larger force, would move up from southwest of Iuka, cutting Price off from van Dorn.

This was a tactic reminiscent of Frederick the Great, but in reverse: the rapid concentration of force enabling the destruction of a dispersed enemy. The tactic worked. On September 19, the Union's Ord attacked Price. The attack was supposed to be coordinated with one by Rosecrans, but Rosecrans botched the whole affair from start to finish. He couldn't get organized in time for a joint attack, and Price, bloodied but hardly beaten, slipped out of his positions around Iuka and joined up with van Dorn.

Grant had been en route to Iuka himself. The plan could still be salvaged, provided Rosecrans set off in hot pursuit. Grant gave him the orders for the pursuit, then rode with him for the first few miles to see that his orders were carried out. The moment he turned back, Rosecrans stopped. It was one of those inexplicable moments that documentary evidence cannot explain.

Whatever Rosecrans's reason for disobeying Grant's orders, it meant that Iuka was another partial victory. The Union was in possession of the battlefield, but the Confederates had gotten away. As Grant had realized when he tried to stir Rosecrans to the pursuit, unless the Confederate forces were physically destroyed, they would be back in short order, spoiling for another battle. Victories weren't scored on points: the other fellow only felt he was defeated when he perceived himself to be whipped.

<hr />

Thus did Grant experience the first of many frustrations of higher command. As armies grew larger, and were spread out over vast expanses of territory, it was no longer possible for the commander to see to every detail. Wellington and Frederick the Great had never had to deal with this problem. They kept their armies close at hand, managed every detail: Wellington once blew up at his medical officer because he had changed the route for the wounded.

Rosecrans was, as Grant said, not a bad general. But at Iuka he failed miserably. Like Napoleon and von Moltke, who had similar problems with their subordinates, Grant had to decide what the mistake warranted.

Whether a mistake or no, Grant stuck with Rosecrans, as he would later stick with Thomas.

The best Grant could do was to set Rosecrans at Corinth with about 18,000 men. Sherman was tied up at Memphis, and Stephen A. Hurlbut at Jackson, Tennessee, an important railhead that was threatened by marauding Confederate cavalry. Grant kept one division with him as reserve, but clearly the numbers were misleading: if Corinth was attacked, Rosecrans was going to have to fend for himself.

Van Dorn made straight for Corinth. He attacked on October 3, driving Rosecrans' men back from one of Halleck's many fortified lines toward a newer one on the outskirts of the town. Unlike the commander at Iuka, Rosecrans was at least willing to fight a defensive battle. By dark, the two sides were worn out.

Now came Grant's countermoves. Jackson, Tennessee, was only sixty miles from Corinth. Grant put his reserves on the train for Corinth. Mindful of what had happened at Iuka, Grant now sent Hurlbut south from Bolivar. Now that van Dorn had committed his forces, he couldn't threaten middle Tennessee, and one or the other of his commanders ought to be able to catch Price from behind.

Grant's wisdom in sending two separate generals to catch van Dorn quickly became evident. McPherson detrained too late the next day to catch the Confederates. Once again, although explicitly ordered to pursue, Rosecrans stayed put and began emitting a stream of self-congratulatory dispatches. But the retreating Confederate forces ran squarely into Hurlbut, and had to double back to the southwest.

Now that the enemy was gone, Rosecrans was all for hot pursuit, but Grant, realizing that the Confederates were digging in at Holly Springs (southwest of Corinth), managed to make him halt. Left to his own devices, Rosecrans would have gotten the core of Grant's army destroyed when he blundered into Price and van Dorn.

Corinth was a victory, although a messy one. Like Iuka, it would have been decisive but for the failures of the local commanders, Rosecrans in particular. After Corinth, Grant should have sacked his recalcitrant, hysteria-prone general, who then went on to a disastrous loss at Chickamauga the following year, which is usually considered, after Gettysburg, to have been the bloodiest battle of the war. That Grant did not sack him reminds us of his one real weakness. He was entirely too charitable towards others, and also forgave mistakes that should have been dealt with quickly and ruthlessly.

+>==<+

Still, Grant had beaten van Dorn and Price sufficiently, and they were no longer in any condition to resume the struggle for northern Mississippi. Grant was free to move on Vicksburg, all the more so since Lincoln had now confirmed him as commander of the Department of the Tennessee. Grant's aim was simple: destroy van Dorn, who was now digging in on the south back of the Tallahatchie River, south of Holly Springs, and then move on Vicksburg. Outflanked, van Dorn retreated towards Oxford.

The fighting in the west during Fall 1862 has been overshadowed completely by the great battles of Lee's Army of Northern Virginia. However, the fighting in the West reveals the extent to which Grant was able to manage forces spread out over a large area. This compensated for the inadequacies of the field commanders, and, above all, blocked determined Confederate attempts to regain control of northern Mississippi and advance into western Tennessee.

In a few short months, Grant had moved from the abyss of despair to the knowledge that he was destined for victory—not that Grant would have used the word *destined*. He would have simply said that he was simply following orders.

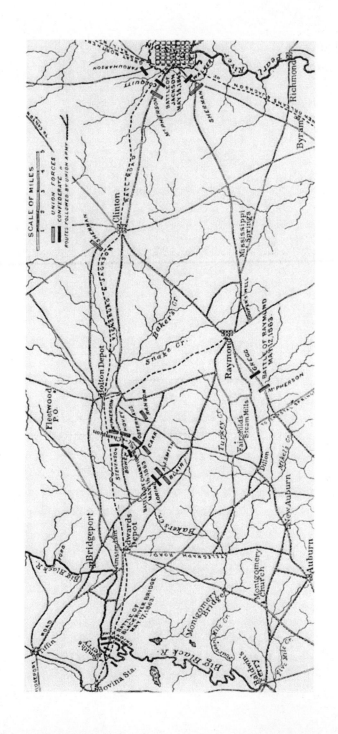

CHAPTER 9

Vicksburg and the
Fall of Mississippi

THE FIGHTING IN NORTHERN MISSISSIPPI HAD BEEN FORCED on
Grant by Halleck's conduct. Now that the Confederates were in disarray,
Grant went back to the central objective of the war in the West: to gain
Union control of the Mississippi River by seizing Vicksburg. Even while he
was fighting off van Dorn and Price, Grant had been planning his next
move, and had repeatedly telegraphed Halleck regarding his intentions.

Everyone realized at some level that Vicksburg was important:
practically speaking it was the last Confederate bastion on the river.
Grant's intention had always been to drive south toward Jackson, cutting Vicksburg off from the rest of the Confederacy before advancing
on the city.

As far as Grant was concerned, this was the only sound approach to Vicksburg, because of basic geography. The distribution of available manpower suggested a move to the south: Union forces were in Tennessee and northern Mississippi, not New Orleans. The rough terrain north of Vicksburg, made impassable by regular overflows of the river, dictated a route through the central axis of the state down to Jackson, Mississippi. From their railroad bases at Jackson, and Iuka, Mississippi, the Union could easily fend off any further Confederate advances, attempts to cut off Grant's army from its base.

To Grant's consternation, however, when he finally got a reply from Halleck, he was told he could do no such thing. In Halleck's view, Grant was doing everything wrong. He must consolidate his forces in Memphis, Halleck wrote him, and from there, advance down the river. This strategy was not only doomed to fail for the reasons just outlined, but it meant abandoning the territory conquered in northern Mississippi.

To this day no one knows whether Halleck was simply ignorant of geography or willfully trying to ensure that Grant would fail. The east bank of the Mississippi above Vicksburg was atrocious country even by the standards of Civil War generals: nothing but forest and swamp, with no roads to speak of. There was a reason why the railroad from Memphis went to Grenada and then down to Jackson rather than through Greenville and then to Vicksburg, the reason was the Yazoo River, which ran parallel to the Mississippi and then merged into it just above Vicksburg.

To add insult to injury, one of Grant's generals, John A. McClernand, had been conducting intrigues in Washington, and had convinced Lincoln that he could take Vicksburg easily. So Lincoln directed the army to put McClernand in charge of the expedition, thus once again reducing Grant to the figurehead he had been after Halleck had taken command and made him his second. In both cases the result was the same: the removal of Grant from direct command of troops in the field.

Lincoln's intervention put Grant in a difficult situation. Halleck was no more in agreement with what Lincoln was doing than Grant was, so there was no point in complaining to him, particularly since every action Halleck had taken had the end result of stripping Grant of troops. Nor was Grant the type of man to go around Halleck and appeal directly to Lincoln—not that it would have done him any good, as the McClernand affair was only one in a long list of misguided presidential interventions with disastrous results.

Worse was still to come. As Grant was forced to withdraw his troops and concentrate them according to Halleck's orders, Confederate cavalry went on a wild rampage up and down the rail lines along the Mississippi. On December 15, horsemen under Confederate General Nathan Bedford Forrest raided Humboldt, Tennessee. Five days later van Dorn launched a massive raid on Holly Springs. Commanded by the same officer who had fled Iuka without firing a shot, the main Union supply depot was abandoned just like Iuka had been. Grant's supply situation was in shambles.

The only bright spot was that the telegraph system had collapsed along with the rail lines, so that McClernand never got the order to assume command, and Sherman, Grant's original choice, was already steaming down the river. Grant's order to Sherman had been brief: he gave him the objective and left it to him how to manage the taking of it. There wasn't much else he could do: Halleck's orders had completely tied his hands, and he couldn't personally lead the force himself, so he had to stand back and let Sherman try to solve the problem on his own, even though Grant had a pretty good idea that it couldn't really be solved. There was no way to get into Vicksburg from the north.

Unfortunately for Sherman, in order to follow Halleck's orders, he had to storm a natural defensive redoubt, the Walnut Hills, basically a bluff with one end anchored by the Mississippi and the other by Chickasaw Bayou. With even a minimally competent defense, the position was impregnable, and the local Confederate commander, Martin Luther Smith, was more than just competent. He had nearly 14,000 men and Sherman had 33,000, but the whole Union plan was suicidal.

Not surprisingly, Sherman's attacks (December 27, 28, 29) achieved nothing, the only surprise being the relatively low Union casualties of about 1,200 killed and wounded. Sherman, having made a valiant effort to obey Halleck's orders, then decided to attack in a more promising place,

Hayne's Bluff. The weather forced a delay, and while Sherman was waiting for it to change, McClernand arrived and took command of what he proposed to call the Army of the Mississippi, despite the fact that most of the state was still in Confederate hands. Having named his force, McClernand then steamed about forty miles up the Arkansas River and attacked the Confederate position at Arkansas Post, Fort Hindman. The fort duly fell, on January 11, 1863. Elated by his great success, McClernand then proposed to take Little Rock, about eighty miles further upstream.

Little Rock, Arkansas, is to the northwest of Vicksburg, Mississippi. McClernand's force was now headed directly away from the objective he had been assigned to capture. There is nothing to suggest the rationale for such behavior, other than McClernand's vainglorious desire to make a name for himself as a great general. As events unfolded at Vicksburg in May 1863, this explanation seems the most probable.

+⇥——⇤+

Grant now did something surprising. He had spent enough time under Halleck's thumb to have sized the man up perfectly. Grant figured that when Halleck heard that McClernand was launching a risky expedition off into the blue, he would be horrified. Sure enough, when told, Halleck promptly authorized Grant to relieve McClernand, and Grant, assuming command himself, and aided by the panic in Washington, settled down to determine how to take Vicksburg.

The panic had a simple cause. On November 7, Lincoln, at Halleck's urging, and largely owing to his manipulations, sacked McClellan from his post as commander of the Army of the Potomac, and named Major General Ambrose Burnside to replace him. Although Burnside was supposedly just the man to carry the war further into Virginia, which Lincoln was still obsessed with, he turned out to be simply another example of disastrous presidential interventions. At the battle of Fredericksburg (December 13, 1862), Burnside outnumbered Lee about three to two, but Lee not only beat him, but he also won the casualty exchange by nearly two to one. With more victories like this, the Confederacy would win the war. What Grant had realized in April about the toughness and competence of the Confederates, Washington was finally beginning to realize.

Grant, who now had Halleck off his case, went back to his original plan. The only way to take Vicksburg was from the east. Initially, the best way to do that was to march straight down the state and then follow the railroad from Jackson to Vicksburg. Now that the Confederates were in control of so much of northern Mississippi, this was no longer possible. By November Grant had concluded that the only sensible advance was from the south, presumably downriver below Vicksburg, all the way from Grand Gulf, as the ground was higher and less swampy between Vicksburg and Natchez.

Although Grant still hadn't figured out how to deal with subordinates like McClernand and Rosecrans, he had entered the war as a very close-mouthed general, and nothing that had happened thus far had made him more loquacious. He didn't hold staff meetings, and he certainly didn't tip his hand. Now he settled down and waited patiently for the dry weather of late spring. The winter had seen remarkably heavy rainfall; campaigning was impossible until the ground finally dried out. But secrecy was vital as well: Joseph Johnston, who was now in command of the West for the Confederacy, was an astute general. If he were to get wind of what Grant intended, he would deploy forces to block him.

Grant hit on a perfect scheme. Just opposite Vicksburg the river formed one of its great loops, the upstream side of the loop being one reason the batteries on the bluff were so ominous. But on the Louisiana side, a complicated system of lakes and bayous existed. With high water, these were navigable, and Grant, no mean civil engineer, figured that with a certain amount of digging, a waterway could be put together that would allow his men to bypass Vicksburg altogether. So he set them to work.

Grant's canal is generally dismissed as pie in the sky, a ridiculous idea, but it existed, and in late March 1863 a steam tug navigated it all the way down to New Carthage. The heavy rainfall of the winter had lifted the level of the river that spring, but by early April, the river was unseasonably low, too low to keep the water level sufficient for use. The problem would only get worse, so Grant began moving troops by land along the Louisiana side. The navy had been trying to clear the stretch of the river below Vicksburg of Confederate craft all spring, and by April they had not only succeeded, but had figured out that they could run by the Vicksburg batteries at night with a good chance of success.

By the end of April two convoys had made a successful run, and two of the three army corps were assembled around New Carthage, about thirty miles below Vicksburg. To mask this end run, Grant ordered one of his cavalry commanders, Colonel Benjamin Grierson, to copy the earlier Confederate raids into Tennessee. On April 17, three cavalry regiments departed LaGrange, Tennessee. They rode almost due south, cut the railroad and telegraph lines connecting Jackson to Meridian, then turned to the southwest. They destroyed the Jackson–New Orleans rail line just south of Hazelhurst, made a dogleg back toward Brookhaven, finally reaching Baton Rouge, Louisiana two weeks later.

Cavalry had been used on similar raids for centuries, but their task had always been the straightforward one of confusion and destruction. Grierson's raid was the first time a major cavalry detachment had been used for strategic deception. But it also gave Grant valuable information about the interior of the state of Mississippi; his eventual advance into that state paralleled Grierson's route out of it.

By the end of April, both Johnston and General John C. Pemberton, now in command at Vicksburg, had divined that Grant had trumped their control of the river, that he had three corps across. On May 1 Grant soundly defeated a hastily thrown-together Confederate force on the road to Port Gibson, which suggested the Union forces were well inland. Further adding to the confusion was a joint Union army-navy offensive on May 3, which destroyed the Confederate position at Grand Gulf. Grant, who had ordered that attack, now made Grand Gulf his temporary headquarters. These actions made Grant look like he was following the Halleck recipe, and that he might reach Vicksburg by Halloween.

The problem that Pemberton and Johnston faced was simple. Vicksburg was not a fort on the grand European model. It had no walls, and its command of the river was a function of some heavy guns parked on the bluff overlooking the river. Although the other three sides all had slopes of differing angles, and presented an attacker with serious difficulties, the position was neither impregnable nor even all that defensible.

The two Confederate generals had no real choice but to try to mount their defense in the field. Their problem was to try to divine Grant's direction. Port Gibson was about thirty miles due south of Vicksburg. If Grant moved upstream, he could be supplied from the river when he reached Warrenton, about ten miles to the south of the city. But the terrain made rapid maneuver impossible. If the Confederates gathered their forces in the wrong place, Grant could slip by them—exactly what he had been planning would happen. Much the same thing happened in May 1940, when the German advance through Belgium traveled south of where the British and French main deployment was, and again in the First Iraq War, when the main allied invasion force went far to the west of Iraqi forces.

It wasn't until May 12, when McPherson's corps reached Raymond, and drove the surprised Confederates back on Jackson, that Johnston and Pemberton realized they'd been duped: Grant was driving on Jackson, not Vicksburg. Johnston's whole plan had been to wait until the true line of Grant's advance on the river fortress was revealed. While Pemberton engaged his forces, Johnston's smaller detachment could attack him from the flank. If both Confederate forces were combined, Grant would be seriously outnumbered.

But Johnston lacked the manpower to fight a battle on his own against Grant. So on May 14, as McPherson's men moved into Jackson, Johnston withdrew. He had been outfoxed: the only practicable route to Vicksburg was along the rail line that ran west from Jackson to the river, which Grant's forces now controlled.

This was a disaster for the Confederates: Pemberton had most of the available troops (there were over 30,000 men at Vicksburg), but Johnston had all the brainpower. The best Pemberton could manage was to occupy a good defensive position at Champion's Hill, just to the west of Jackson, along the rail line. Grant, now directing operations himself, had slightly under 30,000 men (McPherson and McClernand's commands), so Pemberton was greatly outnumbered. This was not an accident: Grant had been carefully directing his detachments so that they could combine quickly into a force large enough to overwhelm any Confederate field army likely to show up.

Still, Champion's Hill (May 16, 1863) was a surprising rout. Grant's troops stormed the position, smothered the Confederate defensive fire, and captured over 2,000 soldiers, together with all of Pemberton's artillery. The key to the victory was that Grant attacked on two sides, troops coming from Jackson catching Pemberton's forces on his left flank.

Pemberton now tried to make a stand on the west side of the Big Black River, the last real obstacle between Grant and the city. Although the position was a good one, the Confederates put up surprisingly little resistance in the face of a determined attack. But by then the whole defense was in a shambles: the bridge across the river, which should have been destroyed early on, was left intact until the end of the battle, when there was a feeble attempt to set fire to it. By May 19, Grant was on the approach to the city.

✦━━✦

Thus far Halleck had been quiet, as he was grappling with the latest Union defeat, Chancellorsville, where, despite being grossly outnumbered (by some accounts nearly two to one), Lee won what most historians consider his finest victory, and launched his second great drive north.

But Grant was no sooner on the move to the siege of Vicksburg than he received an order from Halleck, dated May 11, telling him to go back to Grand Gulf and wait for Major General Nathaniel Banks, who, as commander of the Department of the Gulf, was supposedly going to reinforce him with troops based in New Orleans. Then he was to join in a siege of Port Hudson, and only move on Vicksburg after that had been accomplished. The incident as Grant relates it is a perfect illustration of his style.

> I told the officer that the order came too late, and that Halleck would not give it if he knew our position. The bearer of the dispatch insisted that I ought to obey the order, and was giving argu-

ments to support his position when I heard a great cheering to the right of our line, and, looking in that direction, saw Lawler in his shirt sleeves leading a charge upon the enemy. I immediately mounted my horse and rode in the direction of the charge, and saw no more of the officer who delivered the dispatch; I think not even to this day.[1]

This time Grant was not to be put off. Given the military situation for the Union, Halleck had no choice but to go along.

Although the various markers, plaques, and dozens of monuments and statues covering the Vicksburg battlefield today give visitors the impression that a great battle was fought there, there was very little actual fighting. Having reached the outskirts of the city by May 17, Grant risked an assault on the nineteenth, trying to see if the easy victory at Big Black could be repeated. This was repulsed, but the advance gained valuable jumping-off territory for a future attack, and Grant's local commanders were brimming with confidence, so on May 22 he authorized a second attempt. This failed as well, with substantial casualties, largely owing to McClernand, who claimed his troops had breached the defensive positions in front of them when they actually hadn't, thus encouraging Grant to let the attack continue.[2]

Although most of the losses of the second assault were not Grant's fault, the failure of the assaults has led to his being roundly criticized. But his reasoning was impeccable. Johnston was gathering Confederate forces to the east; thus far Pemberton's forces had shown little aptitude for defending good natural positions, and seemed demoralized. But the reason most important to Grant was this: "The troops believed they could carry the works in their front, and would not have worked so patiently in the trenches if they had not been allowed to try."[3]

Therein lies one of the secrets of Grant's generalship: he realized that his men could not be treated like the soldiers of an earlier era, a point he made early on in discussing Shiloh. Although new to warfare, they were intelligent and independent; it was necessary to let them learn, and only then would they follow and submit to any sort of military discipline. Now that the Union troops could see there was no chance of a direct assault succeeding without much more work, they settled down to a siege.

Grant disliked the idea of sieges. Like Wellington, he preferred to attack his enemies in the field. But Grant also knew when to be patient. Pemberton's position was unsustainable: Vicksburg didn't have enough food to feed its garrison for any length of time, and the city was now totally surrounded. What Grant aimed to do was to make Pemberton think that he would shortly be under a sustained artillery bombardment that would destroy the city, together with his garrison. Grant didn't have any heavy siege guns, but he borrowed some from the navy, whose bombardments of the city had thus far proven largely ineffectual.

Thus set up, Grant was in a position to conduct active siege operations, and by the end of June he was preparing for an all-out assault, supported by the heavy rifled artillery he had borrowed from the navy. The assault was scheduled for July 6, but it was not to be. Pemberton asked for terms on July 1, and the city surrendered on the fourth. Although in legend much is made of Grant's demands for unconditional surrender, in fact he was quite reasonable. The garrison that Pemberton surrendered was 29,306 men. By letting them go on parole, Grant saved his command the enormous logistical expense of maintaining them. Additionally, he felt that once beaten, they would serve as effective propagandists for the Union cause, albeit unintentionally. Desertions were a problem for both sides, but increasingly the Confederate forces were leaking men like a sieve—anything that could be done to encourage this hemorrhaging was shrewd business.

Coming on the heels of a string of major Union disasters, the fall of Vicksburg should have made Grant an overnight hero. Alone among the Union field commanders, Grant had an unbroken string of triumphs, and his campaign for Vicksburg is one of the more phenomenal feats in military history. There had been no less than nine separate engagements in his approach to the city; his men had won every one of them, at the cost of less than 3,500 casualties. Grant and his men had occupied the state capital, and now they had the last remaining strongpoint on the river as well.

Once again, however, events conspired against Grant. The cost of the war was beginning to cause serious unrest in the North. Within the same week as the surrender of Vicksburg, the draft riots broke out in New York. At precisely the same time, news was received of another horrific battle, Gettysburg. By any reckoning, Gettysburg was a bloody battle: the Union lost one out of every five soldiers engaged, the Confederates three out of every ten. It was very well to call Gettysburg a Union victory, and it was, but possession of the battlefield on such bloody terms, coming after repeated heavy losses in the previous eleven months of fighting, was sobering. For the North, perhaps too sobering, particularly since there was a growing feeling that the government had grossly mismanaged the war.

Halleck's feelings about Grant's victory are not known, but Lincoln, to his credit, made his crystal clear. After outlining his own rather eccentric views on what Grant should have done, he concluded: "You were right and I was wrong."[4] It was the only time a president apologized to one of his generals.

CHAPTER 10

Winning the War in the West

WITH THE FALL OF VICKSBURG, UNION IRONCLADS controlled the entire length of the Mississippi River, all the way to the Gulf of Mexico, thus severing the Confederate heartland from Louisiana and Texas, a valuable source of men and supplies. But Grant had always seen this objective simply as a stepping stone, the prelude to a concerted attack on the Confederacy. He had long since come to the conclusion that the only way to win the war was by taking the fighting into the South, beating its armies, and occupying its territory.

Every other general Union by now agreed with this insight; the problem was how to go about it. Grant had been studying the problem for almost two years, and it seemed to him that the Union strategies so far had been difficult to execute, simply because of the logistics of advancing through the dense mountains and rough terrain that formed the natural northern frontier of the Confederacy between the Virginia coast and Chattanooga. Union efforts could have succeeded, but as they often had not, a different plan was called for.

New Orleans had already fallen into Union hands and Vicksburg, which was the one remaining obstacle, had been captured. The way had been cleared for an operation that Grant believed would bring the war to a speedy end. What he envisioned was a series of coordinated thrusts into the South from three directions: one from Tennessee and Kentucky, one from Mississippi, and the most important one, an advance up through Alabama and Georgia. With control of the river, all three thrusts could easily be supported.

The thrust up into Alabama and Georgia was the most important, because it would stretch the Confederate forces in the West to the breaking point. Joseph Johnston, the Confederate general in charge of the area, had enough men to beat off any one concentrated offensive. In December 1862 Braxton Bragg, although greatly outnumbered, had brought the Northern thrust into eastern Tennessee to a dead halt at the Battle of Murfreesboro, one of the bloodier battles of the Civil War.

Grant anticipated the Union checks on the battlefield. The Confederates were simply too good on the battlefield to risk everything on a single victory. Even if the Union won, their armies would be too weakened to follow through on the victory. Nor would two simultaneous thrusts (one from Mississippi and one from Tennessee) do any good. Given how the railroads ran in the region, all Johnston had to do was draw a line along each advance, stand at the point the lines intersected, and shuttle reinforcements to whichever place needed help.

The idea of two simultaneous thrusts was unworkable, as it would give Johnston the advantage of interior lines of communication. He could always get from one threatened point to the other faster than his opponents could. In both world wars, the Germans did exactly the same thing, moving reinforcements to the point where the allies threatened.

Grant saw the solution perfectly, as did commanders Joseph Joffre and Eisenhower in the following century: attack on a broad enough scale, and the enemy would not be able to take advantage of his interior lines, and would have to deploy all his troops simply to keep up the fight.

In Europe, the only practical way to achieve this advantage was to attack on a broad front, which was not possible in America. But Grant saw that geography now gave the Union a great advantage. With control of the Mississippi Valley and New Orleans, an offensive could be mounted from the gulf coast as well. In essence, this was the same plan the British government favored in both world wars, the difference being that in those cases, geography worked to the Allied disadvantage. Neither Italy nor the Balkans was favorable theaters of operation, owing to the mountainous terrain and the heavily urbanized transportation infrastructure. In the case of the Civil War, Grant now saw that the landscape of southern Mississippi and Alabama was ideally suited to offensive operations. It would allow the deployment of large forces that could live off the land as they advanced.

Johnston would be faced with an insurmountable problem. He lacked the manpower to fight on two widely separate fronts. But he could not choose not to fight, because a force moving up from Mobile would quickly reach Atlanta, in northern Georgia. But if he stood and fought, the other Union forces would surround him, and cut him off from the rest of the Confederacy. If he retreated, trying to preserve his army intact, he would have to abandon the greater part of the South, which would quickly be reduced to a few states along the coast.

Either way, Grant reckoned that the war would end quickly, and that Johnston would probably opt to keep his army intact, and so would simply retreat further east. But that would be the end of the Confederacy, because its armies absolutely depended on supplies being produced in Alabama and Georgia. So Grant's plan was Vicksburg on a continental scale, and, he hoped, with a similar result: a massive surrender with a minimal amount of bloodshed.

Keeping Johnston on the defensive appealed to Grant for another reason. As he would confess after the war, Grant had a much higher opinion of Johnston than he did of Lee: "I never ranked Lee as high as some others of the army. . . . I never had as much anxiety when he was at my front as when Joe Johnston was in front."[1] Having to contend with a war on three fronts would keep Johnston busy, keep him from breaking loose.

In fact, it would present Johnston with a problem that couldn't be solved. Absent a great numerical advantage, there was basically no way a defense could succeed against attacks from three sides, as the Polish high command would realize in 1939. For the Poles, the only hope lay in French and British attacks directed at Germany that would force it to move troops back into Germany proper. When the French and the British did not attack, Poland was doomed, and fell in six weeks. Similarly, nobody was going to come to Johnston's aid, and he would soon be defeated.

The Confederacy would probably have held out for more than six weeks, but it is worth noting that in 1870, during the Franco-Prussian War, the French, faced with a roughly similar situation (their capital surrounded, their armies dispersed and cut off from sources of supply), surrendered after only seven months.[2]

The operation was more than feasible. General Nathaniel Banks already had 40,000 men in New Orleans; Sherman and Rosecrans had even larger armies already in place. Grant promptly proposed his strategy to Halleck, who just as promptly turned it down. Lincoln, still fixated on east Tennessee, now had another fear.

In 1862, the French, quick to benefit from American troubles, had sent an army to Mexico with the ultimate aim of creating a European monarchy there. Lincoln was convinced that France might stir up further mischief, either by recognizing the Confederacy as a belligerent, or even possibly by invading the United States. This was a good example of grand strategic thinking gone berserk, but Halleck dutifully ordered Grant to send an army corps to New Orleans to reinforce General Banks's Army of the Gulf, which would supposedly deter the French from invading Texas. Then Grant was told to send every man he could spare to reinforce Rosecrans, who was supposed to complete the conquest of Tennessee by taking Chattanooga.

Grant's judgment about the futility of engaging in one-on-one battles proved correct. On September 19, 1863, Braxton Bragg's army mauled Union forces under Rosecrans at the Battle of Chickamauga, an engagement that was, after Gettysburg, the bloodiest battle of the Civil War. As it was, what was left of Rosecrans's army retreated to Chattanooga, a basically indefensible spot ringed by mountains from which Bragg's Confederates could dominate the position, including control of the approaches and, therefore, the supply of food and provisions.

At first, Lincoln simply moved to send in more men: Joseph Hooker from the Army of the Potomac with two corps, together with McPherson and Sherman from Grant's command. Belatedly, the president realized that basic geography made his ideas impractical: Grant's generals would have to travel over hundreds of miles of single-track railroad, and Hooker was nearly fifty miles to the south of Chattanooga.

So on October 3, Lincoln took what in retrospect seems an obvious step: he put Grant in command of all the Union armies west of the Allegheny Mountains, and sent Edwin Stanton, his secretary of war, out to meet him as Grant traveled toward Chattanooga. Three armies were subordinate to this command, technically called the Military Division of the Mississippi (a belated recognition of its importance): Tennessee, Cumberland, and Ohio.

For the first time, Grant was allowed to choose his subordinates. Grant had always had a very high opinion of George Thomas, one that has continued in posterity. Fourteen months later, Thomas would win one of the relatively few decisive Union victories of the war, thus amply justifying Grant's opinion of him. So Grant chose Thomas to lead the Army of the Cumberland, and Rosecrans was dispatched to the rear.

The officer Grant most trusted was Sherman, who had been with him at both Shiloh and Vicksburg. Sherman had the one quality that Thomas lacked, the quality that Grant prized most of all: the ability to move rapidly. The choice of Sherman to head the Army of the Tennessee gives us an insight into Grant's strategic thinking: his ideas about multiple offensive thrusts might still be workable, and if they were, Sherman would be the man to succeed. He was the only man Grant had confidence in to carry out such a thrust with the requisite speed, just as Grant had confidence in Thomas to hold fast and block any sudden offensive moves by Johnston.

Grant decided to let Ambrose Burnside stay on as commander of the Army of the Ohio, probably because Lincoln had given him that command after his brief and unhappy tenure in command of the Army of the Potomac and the disastrous loss at Fredericksburg (December 13–14, 1862). All three appointments put Burnside in positions far above his abilities, but by October 1863 there were very few first-rate Union generals around, and Grant deferred to Lincoln's decision.

The immediate problem that the Union soldiers cooped up in Chattanooga faced was that their supply routes had been cut off. Confederate gunners on Lookout Mountain could interdict the Tennessee River as well as the railroad that ran into the city from Bridgeport, about thirty miles to the west. But when Grant reached Chattanooga on October 23, he discovered that Thomas's engineering officer had worked out a plan that would finesse the Confederate stranglehold on the city. Downstream from the city there were two ferry crossings. If the ferries were replaced by temporary pontoon bridges, a supply route would be created that lay outside of the range of the Confederate guns, and this new route could easily be protected by Hooker's forces. Grant directed Hooker's forces to position themselves between Lookout Mountain and the river.

Now that the supply problem had been solved, Grant immediately turned his mind to dislodging Bragg's forces from their positions on the heights overlooking the city. Although at first blush the Confederate position seemed well nigh impregnable, it had a weakness. All the Confederate supplies had to go through the railhead at Chickamauga station, about five miles east of Missionary Ridge.

Grant had fought Bragg at Shiloh, and so he knew that he was an aggressive general, not one to sit around idly and wait to be attacked. Nor was he about to come down from Missionary Ridge and try to storm into the city. His best option, Grant considered, was to try to draw the Union forces away from the city, and the best way to do that was to go after Burnside's Army of the Ohio.

But this, Grant thought, would play directly into his hands. Bragg was already outnumbered. The practical consequence of that would be a lack of reserves to cover possible Union breakthroughs if they attacked the main Confederate line on Missionary Ridge and Lookout Mountain. Absent reserves, the only way that Bragg could save his railhead was by deploying troops from that line, thus weakening his defenses.

Bragg promptly sent Lieutenant General James Longstreet and his 20,000 men north to crush Burnside, as he judged Longstreet could probably defeat the Army of the Ohio, or at least threaten them to the extent that Grant would have to move north. His logic was impeccable: every time a Confederate force moved into the Union, or appeared to be poised to make that move, Washington promptly began moving Union forces to try to counter the advance, and each time, the result was to prolong the war, since the armies thus diverted were unable to carry the fight into the South. Given that the South's best hope for winning was to prolong the struggle as long as possible, this strategy was logical, and so far it had been quite successful.

But Grant refused to be distracted. He knew that he could beat Bragg before Longstreet could destroy Burnside, and that when Bragg's forces retreated, back to the southeast, Longstreet would have no choice but to follow. Besides, the same railhead that supplied Bragg had to support Longstreet as well. Seize the railhead and the whole Confederate position would collapse.

Grant's plan, then, was to deceive Bragg into thinking that his main attack was delivered by Hooker to his left flank (Lookout Mountain) and by Thomas against Missionary Ridge, the center of his position. But the real thrust would come from Sherman, who would secretly move to the north and head straight for the railhead and Tunnel Hill. Since Grant had twice as many men, he could tie Bragg down by attacking all across the front, prevent him from sending reinforcements to the real point of the attack.

Although deceptively simple, Grant's plan for the attack revealed an entirely new approach to fighting a battle. The idea of a successful flank attack was hardly new. Turn the enemy's position and he would be forced to withdraw; otherwise he would be surrounded. Grant's innovation was this: Sherman's move around Bragg's right flank, anchored on Missionary Ridge, was not designed to destroy Lieutenant General William Hardee's men on the ridge, but to compel them to abandon the position entirely. Grant saw that the ridge was irrelevant; the prize was the railhead. It was not as though Bragg failed to realize this; Grant aimed to have Sherman's deployment across the river kept secret, so that by the time Bragg saw the threat, it would be too late to stop.

The idea of overloading the enemy's defensive line so that he was unable to counter any breakthrough would be used repeatedly in both world wars, and on a grand scale; perhaps the most successful example was the Allied Normandy assault in June 1944, as both Eisenhower and Montgomery saw that for the assault to succeed they not only had to project an offensive along a broad front, but they had to confuse the opposition about the exact direction of the invasion itself. But Grant's particular combination of tactics and objectives here was unique, and was certainly the first instance of an attack whose success would be measured not by the traditional battlefield victory but by whether the attackers gained an objective not known in previous wars.

It is generally accepted in armies that no plan survives the first shot, but beyond that, there was no way Bragg could handle three major attacks simultaneously; at some point he would have to weaken one part of the line to keep another part from collapsing. Something would have to give. When the attack began, on November 23, this was exactly what happened.

+>===<+

Sherman's progress was much slower than anticipated. But when Bragg realized that this was where the main thrust would fall, he had no choice but to thin out the Lookout Mountain defenders and send them toward Tunnel Hill. In response, Grant ordered Sherman to attack in force on November 25, in conjunction with a strong attack against Missionary Ridge, his aim being to stretch Bragg to the breaking point by forcing him to detach more troops to meet these new simultaneous offensives.

Thomas's men had already taken a lower line on the ridge, and now they pressed home their attack, advancing all the way to the forward Confederate line, where they were met by a hail of fire from the main defenses above them. Their objective had been the forward position: all Grant had intended was to keep the pressure on until Sherman could overpower his opposition and move on the railhead.

But Thomas's men, sensing victory, and realizing, in Grant's words, "that the Union soldier nearest the enemy was in the safest position," swept over the crest, "thus effectually carrying out my orders of the 18th for the battle and of the 25th for this charge"[3]

As the Confederate center collapsed, the commanders on the wings, realizing they were in danger of being cut off from retreat, abandoned the field. This time there was a serious pursuit. Sherman went north, where Burnside was being outmaneuvered, and chased Longstreet back into the mountains. In two days Grant had cleared east Tennessee, an objective dear to Lincoln's heart, and one that had frustrated Lincoln for years.

Storming the ridge was not without its cost: Grant's army had suffered nearly 6,000 casualties. Most of the Confederate losses were prisoners; actual combat losses in killed and wounded were about 2,500. But previous Union generals had lost twice as many men, and the battle as well: Rosecrans had over 16,000 casualties at Chickamauga and Pope had the same number at Second Bull Run. For the third time, Grant had managed a brilliant recovery from the strategic imbroglios that had thus far been the most conspicuous of Halleck and Lincoln's achievements. Belatedly, the tide of opinion was beginning to turn in Grant's favor. In December, Congress passed a vote of thanks to Grant and his soldiers, and ordered that a medal be struck.

CHAPTER 11

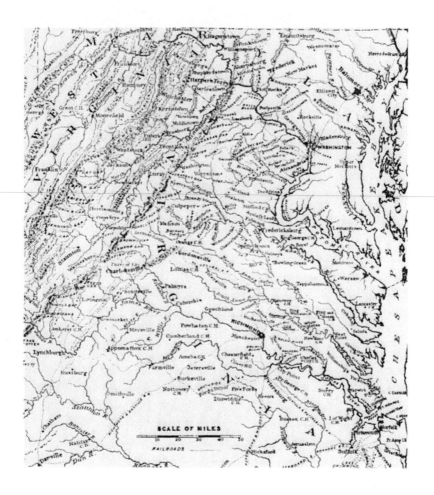

The Defeat of Robert E. Lee

GRANT NOW TURNED ONCE MORE TO THE PLAN he had pushed six months earlier: three great thrusts into the Confederacy, with the decisive one moving up into Georgia from the Alabama coast. The problem with having seized Chattanooga was that movement further east was impractical, owing to the terrain. Chattanooga was an important rail junction, and its loss was a blow to the Confederacy, but it was basically nothing but a symbol, and one that existed primarily in Lincoln's mind. By contrast, a rapid advance up from Mobile would surround Lee and Johnston, and quickly lead to their surrender, as the Union armies would be sitting across their home base and blocking their supplies.

Once again, Lincoln and Halleck ignored his plan, so Grant contented himself with letting Sherman clear out the rest of Mississippi and move toward a confrontation with Joseph Johnston, now based in Georgia and in command of the Confederacy's western armies. For the next three months there was a lull in the war. Although in Virginia both sides had substantial forces totaling over 100,000 men, Mine Run (November 17–December 1) was a minor engagement. The Union was playing to a Confederate strength: the more time that passed, the better the Confederacy's chances of survival.

The inconclusive skirmish at Mine Run spoke to the heart of a serious problem affecting Union forces in the East: repeated confrontations with Lee, who always whacked them hard, had turned the officers and men of the Army of the Potomac into a timid and indecisive force, had given them an almost superstitious regard for Lee's abilities. That fear, coupled with the poor leadership of the senior officers, would prove a thorny problem for Grant in the months ahead.

And now the time was at hand. On March 3, 1864, Lincoln made a momentous decision. He appointed Grant commander of all the Union forces in the field. Nearly three years into the war, the North finally had a supreme commander who deserved the confidence of the president. And, once he had settled on Grant, Lincoln abandoned any attempt to direct military affairs. He let Grant run the war, and backed him to the hilt. The year 1864 would prove to be the time of his finest achievement, as it would for Grant.

The grand strategic problem Grant faced is simple to describe, but exceedingly difficult to solve. The Confederacy was down to an intractable core with substantial forces in the field, and showed no signs of being ready to quit, while the Union electorate was increasingly wobbly. There was a very real chance that the Democrats would prevail in the fall elections, and end the war on any terms they could manage. As one of the best of the basic historical surveys of the period puts it,

> War weariness was pervasive in the North by the late summer [of 1864], and a discouraged Lincoln was convinced that he stood no

chance of reelection in November. His own party was divided by the charges of the antislavery leaders that Lincoln was too lenient in his reconstruction policy, and Democrats were damning him for unnecessarily prolonging the war by making emancipation a precondition for reunion.[1]

The political question then was the same one George C. Marshall would face in the Second World War and that we face today in the war on terror: how long can a democracy fight a war? Marshall, like Alexis de Tocqueville before him, was dubious that a democracy had the willpower to fight a long war, and was of the opinion that as any war dragged on, there would be a growing swell of voices counseling retreat, withdrawal, or surrender. The political part of the equation seemingly trumped the military one.

But the military problem was equally difficult to solve. Joseph Johnston had a large Confederate army still in the field, while Lee, a master of defensive warfare, was settled in his home ground, northern Virginia. In reality, he was now too weak to brush past the Army of the Potomac and move on Washington, but by this point panic had completely conquered reality. In theory, the Union's advantage in manpower should have made the problem easy to resolve. But thus far, Washington had failed to capitalize on its numerical superiority: giving Banks 40,000 men and keeping him in Louisiana to guard against a hypothetical French threat makes the case perfectly. The government's only solution was to call for more men, but this unpopular move played into the hands of the Democratic Party, already gearing up to run against Lincoln and the Republicans on the charge that they had fatally mismanaged the war.

So Grant now had to consider grand strategy at the highest level, where the political and the military were intermingled. The question Grant had to answer was not how to win a battle or a campaign, but how to win the war as quickly as possible. His idea about a series of coordinated thrusts was still sound, it offered the best chance of victory: the difficulty was that he now lacked the manpower to put it into effect with any speed. As a result, Grant would be forced to put together a plan of action based on the resources he already had with Sherman and with the Army of the Potomac.

Grant's idea for the way to win with the least loss of life was to separate the two main Confederate armies, each from the other, and both from their base. In this reckoning, Richmond was the lodestar of the North's legions of armchair generals and naïve politicians (and the army's high command). The objective was Lee, who had repeatedly demonstrated that he could maneuver out of whatever trap his opponents thought they had him in and then thrash them hard. And in the western reaches, there was room for enormous armies to maneuver. Given enough men, Sherman could net Johnston, or at least starve him out, now that the Union controlled Atlanta; or for that matter, simply ignore him and seal off Lee from the rest of the Confederacy. If Sherman had enough men, he could manage that, and still have the forces necessary to fight off Johnston should he finally decide he had no choice but to give battle.

+‑‑‑‑+

Grant quickly found that he had much more than a strategic problem heavily weighted toward political consequences. He also had a personnel problem of the first order. Grant had confidence in only a few of the senior commanders: Sherman, whom he named to succeed him at the Department of the Mississippi; McPherson, who replaced Sherman with the Army of the Tennessee; and Thomas, with the Army of the Cumberland. Initially, Grant professed a high opinion of George Meade, the commander of the Army of the Potomac, but it is doubtful he retained that judgment once they were working in the field together.[2]

As for the others, they were, in the dry understatement of General Marshall-Cornwall, "a poor lot, but many of them had to be retained for political reasons."[3] Armies often go to war with peacetime generals who are incapable of adjusting to wartime conditions, but the case of the Union army in 1864 was truly unique. To make matters worse, in most cases congressional or presidential politics was involved. Grant was rightly wary of rooting his generals out, and had to wait until their mismanagement became obvious, as had been the case with McClernand earlier.

Although Grant would find competent commanders at the lower levels, and give them important commands, in spring 1864 he very much had to put together a plan that relied on the manpower in the field and the men who commanded them. But putting together ambitious plans and then executing them quickly was a task at which Grant excelled. He stripped his August 1863 plan down still further, reasoning that if he expanded the theater of operations to include the entire Confederacy, he could manage with the forces he had.

+▷══◁+

Like all of Grant's plans, this one was simple: he would personally fix Lee in northern Virginia, and so keep him either from slipping away and wreaking havoc in the North or (worse) joining with Johnston. Meanwhile, Sherman would pin down the other Confederate army still in the field, Joseph Johnston's. If both moves happened simultaneously, neither Confederate general would be able to come to the aid of the other, and neither would be able to make further offensive moves.

Since Lee was on his home ground, Grant had more confidence in Sherman's besting Johnston than he did in the Army of the Potomac defeating Lee outright. But even if Sherman couldn't destroy Johnston outright, the Confederate forces in the west were now too far inside the Confederacy to pose a threat to the North. There were simply too many miles between them and Kentucky and Ohio. Grant figured that the best they could manage would be Nashville.

Moreover, in order to do that, Johnston would have to divide his forces and abandon some key part of the Confederacy, as he lacked the manpower to defend it. But by now, with the Union in control of the entire Mississippi River Valley, the Confederacy could ill afford to lose any more of its territory. The core that was left in Georgia and Alabama was the only real source of supplies for the Confederate forces in the field. Lee's Army of Northern Virginia had long since stripped Virginia bare. If Lee's men were unable to be supplied from the central South, Lee would be forced to surrender.

But Grant went back one step further: in order for Sherman to prevail against Johnston, Lee had to be penned up where he was, and so far, no Union general had managed to do this. So Grant took an unprecedented step. Even though he was in command of all the Union armies in the field, he moved his personal headquarters so as to be sitting on top of the forces in Maryland and Virginia. He had decided that the only way to win was for him to direct both campaigns simultaneously.

In Virginia, his aim was simple: he would pound Lee continuously, never letting up, until he was sure that the Army of Northern Virginia was too battered to take to the field and go on the offensive, and too threatened to be able to send aid elsewhere. But in order to manage that feat, Grant had to get the Army of the Potomac to keep on fighting. This was no easy task. By May 1864, the officers and men of that army were terrorized by Lee, who always managed to beat them one way or another, and who seemed invincible.[4]

This led to one of Grant's few outbursts. When a general (apparently the excitable Meade) came running up to him in a panic, explaining that he knew what Lee would do to turn the battle to his advantage, Grant

> rose to his feet, took his cigar out of his mouth, turned to the officer, and replied, with a degree of animation which he seldom manifested: "Oh, I am heartily tired of hearing what Lee is going to do. Some of you always seem to think he is suddenly going to turn a double somersault, and land in our rear and on both our flanks at the same time. Go back to your command, and try to think what we are going to do ourselves, instead of what Lee is going to do."[5]

Grant's reaction to bad news can best be described as a confident indifference: no reverse was so disastrous that it could not quickly be set right. Besides, as he had noted early on in the war: chances were the other fellow was in just as bad a shape. This was Grant's leadership style in a nutshell: a calm and taciturn confidence, the only instances of animation manifesting themselves almost as a parental irritation caused by someone else's hysteria.

Grant's reproof occurred during the Wilderness campaign (May 4–6, 1864), the first serious trial of arms between Grant and Lee, followed immediately by the Battle of Spotsylvania Court House (May 8–18). Although generally treated as though they were two separate engagements, like those that followed in June (Cold Harbor, June 1–12; Petersburg, June 15–July 31) the two May engagements were actually separate segments of one continuous battle.

The details of these two bloody fights—and the losses incurred—have obscured the success of Grant's strategy. In the May fighting, Grant had killed and wounded of nearly 50,000 men. Lee's losses were substantially less, perhaps half that.[6]

By mid-June, Grant had accomplished two things. He had fixed Lee in place and kept him on the defensive while Sherman developed his thrust into the center of the Confederacy. He had also completely reversed the psychological attitudes of both sides. In his dispatches, Grant did not claim victories, but instead said that over the course of the fighting—which he correctly described as being very heavy—the results were consistently "favorable." On May 26, he wrote that

> Lee's army is really whipped. The prisoners we take now show it, and the action of his army shows it unmistakably. A battle with them outside of entrenchments cannot be had. Our men feel that they have gained the *morale* over the enemy, and attack him with confidence. I may be mistaken, but I feel that our success over Lee's army is already assured.[7]

By and large Grant's assessment of the Confederates was accurate: Lee stayed on the defensive. The effect Grant's personality had on the Union side is remarkable. The erratic but brilliant correspondent Sylvanus Cadwallader sums this up perfectly. On the night of May 5, he was unable to sleep. Two days of fighting had been disastrous, and the unusually sensitive journalist was deeply depressed. Nearby, Grant was dozing peacefully in a chair, seemingly asleep.

> In a short time, however, he straightened up in the chair and finding that I was not asleep, commenced a pleasant chatty conversation upon indifferent subjects. Neither of us alluded to what was

uppermost in our mind for more than half an hour. I then remarked that if we were to get any sleep that night it was time we were in our tents. . . . He smilingly assented. . . . and entered his tent. It was the grandest mental sunburst of my life. I had suddenly emerged from the slough of despond, to the solid bed-rock of unwavering faith. . . . [8]

By the time fighting was renewed, in June, Lee's army had basically become a garrison force. Lee had no choice but to dig in at Petersburg. By so doing, he essentially forfeited what had historically been his great advantage over his opponents: brilliant maneuvers. And that was precisely Grant's aim.

Lee's losses in May had weakened him, particularly in officers. If he moved into the field and went on the offensive, he'd risk being annihilated. If he stayed put, defending Richmond, his army would atrophy, and he would lose his traditional advantage over his enemy. It was the best of a bad choice. But Lee had now lost control over the course of the war. He lacked the resources to win it, could only hang on and hope that Confederate Brigadier General John Hood would manage to destroy Sherman.

⊹⊱━━⊰⊹

Grant kept pushing relentlessly. Only bad weather had aborted a continuation of that bloody May, and now, at Petersburg, Grant settled down for a protracted siege. Never one to settle for a draw if he could win outright, Grant authorized the construction of a great mine beneath the Confederate lines. The work was started on June 25, and exploded on July 30.

In this one particular, the Civil War really was a precursor to the First World War. The Germans and the French both used mines planted beneath the enemy positions by means of tunnels from early 1915 on, and the British and Canadians then copied the technique, which was not repeated after the end of the First World War.

The aftermath of the Petersburg mine explosion should have warned the generals of the First World War why mine warfare was unworkable. The resulting crater was too deep and wide for the advancing infantry to cross—a problem that would reoccur in later wars. Moreover, once again, the local commanders were unprepared to deal with the situation. Grant himself had to wade into the melee and order the assault called off. Burnside, whose Ninth Corps had been charged with the advance, was finally sacked.

There were false alarms and some very real threats during the fall—enough to keep Washington on edge—but Grant was basically right: Lee wasn't going to come out and fight. In terms of scale and importance, there was only one major battle between Petersburg in July 1864 and the Appomattox campaign in late March 1865, and that was Nashville (December 15–16, 1864). As Grant and Sherman had both reckoned, Hood had made for that city, in a last desperate bid to turn the war around by invading Tennessee and Kentucky.

Although Lee and the Army of Northern Virginia are always seen as the embodiment of the last stand, the truth is that the honors should go to Hood. Outnumbered almost two to one, he nevertheless tried his best. Back in Virginia, Grant kept trying to get Thomas to move to the attack, and got so aggravated he finally sent Brigadier General John "Black Jack" Logan to Nashville with orders to relieve him. By the time Logan arrived, Thomas had (finally) attacked and beaten Hood decisively, thus ending the war in the west.

This affair—Grant riding Thomas to move to the attack—is almost always turned around, as though Thomas was right in resisting orders and Grant was wrong in pushing him too hard. Thomas was a stout defensive commander, but previously he had been as slow as Buell, as reluctant to pursue as Rosecrans. Would he have attacked in December had Grant not been riding him mercilessly? There's little in the way of convincing evidence to the contrary.

+≻•≺+

Belatedly, in February 1865, Jefferson Davis made Lee the supreme commander of all Confederate forces, but Lee, bottled up in Virginia, had no control over what forces remained, and precious few under his own command. Nevertheless he showed no signs of quitting the war, and out in

Georgia, Joseph Johnston was organizing the remains of the Confederacy's shattered armies. So at the end of March, Grant moved to a final campaign. He had 112,000 men, to Lee's 49,000. In a week of sporadic fighting, the Union lost about 9,000 men. But Lee's army was melting, largely owing to desertions. Everyone knew the war was lost, and finally Lee himself admitted it.

The surrender at Appomattox Court House was not the end of the Civil War, technically speaking. Johnston hadn't yet surrendered (although he did so shortly thereafter), and there were isolated pockets of resistance scattered throughout the South. Jefferson Davis himself wanted to continue the fight to the bitter end. But with Lee's surrender, the war was effectively over. Grant had won it. He was probably the last of the great generals about whom Napoleon's maxim—that the general is all, the masses nothing—would be true. After the Civil War, warfare would change dramatically. Great generals would no longer wade into the Petersburg crater and give orders. Grant was both the last and best of the classical great commanders.

CHAPTER 12

Grant's Genius

GRANT MAY BE FAIRLY COMPARED WITH THE GREAT GENERALS of Europe, and the comparison is an illuminating one. Frederick the Great and Napoleon both won their greatest victories in the middle of their careers. Towards the end they were not nearly so successful.

After Borodino, which was hardly one of Napoleon's triumphs, he endured Lützen, Dresden, and Leipzig, the last putting him temporarily into exile. Waterloo was really a postscript to a brilliant run of victories that had already begun to wither. The real glory days of his generalship were a decade earlier: Austerlitz, Friedland, Aspern-Essling, and Wagram. By contrast, Grant prevailed steadily and against all comers. The closest he came to a setback was The Wilderness in May 1864, but as we have seen, an inconclusive victory on the basis of the casualty exchange was ultimately not a real victory for Lee.

A better comparison for Grant would be with Wellington, arguably the most distinguished general his country has ever produced, and, like Grant, one who never tasted defeat. Napoleon thought him simply a colonial general, but Wellington not only beat every French general sent to Spain against him, he finally beat Napoleon himself. Like Grant, he was saddled with subordinates of only marginal competence, and was consequently forced to often undo the mistakes of his own commanders. And both men went on to the highest elected office their country could offer.

There is another point: both generals came out of democracies, free societies in which they believed deeply and sought to uphold. Napoleon was a despot, Frederick the Great merely an enlightened one. Curiously, Grant and Wellington are clearly the most undervalued of the four, when by any logical system they should be the most praised.

There are two important differences, however, between these two groups of generals. Napoleon was truly beaten by a great coalition. The Prussians had a major part in the victory of Waterloo, and the French army of that battle was not the army that had entered the bloody engagements of fall 1813. As such things are generally reckoned, and given Napoleon's army of hagiographers, this lessens Wellington's triumph. But after 1863, Grant was the guiding spirit of the Union Army. He did not step in at the end to finish his enemy off, but harried him mercilessly until he quit the war.

At the same time, he was a functioning supreme commander, directing a dozen armies spread over an immense geographical region, all of them requiring precise instructions to achieve one goal, the destruction of the Confederacy. Wellington's actual command never exceeded 40,000 men, about the maximum that one general could direct and control personally in those days. Although Napoleon did direct immense armies spread out over Europe, there was no need for him to coordinate any common strategy and ensure that it was followed. The war in Spain, for example, was a struggle that had next to nothing to do with what was going on in Central Europe—one reason why Wellington's career has consistently been undervalued by military historians. Grant had to make sure that all these dispersed forces did what they were supposed to do. Given the history of Union generals, this was clearly not an easy task.

Grant can easily stand these comparisons; in fact, in almost every instance, he comes out the best of the group. He was, for instance, the only one of the four great captains mentioned above who had to deal with the impact of radically new military technologies, and the only one to labor under the handicaps of inexpert superiors. At certain points Wellington's situation came close to Grant's, but the Englishman had the inestimable advantage of family connections in high political places, while Grant had only his fellow native of Illinois, Congressman Elihu Washburne.

Some of Grant's best generalship came as he salvaged disasters created by Halleck in Northern Mississippi in 1862 and by Lincoln's amateurish insistence on the Tennessee offensives the following year. In both situations Grant was able to cobble together victories out of potential disasters: Corinth, Iuka, Chattanooga.

Finally, there is the matter of the opposition that Grant had to beat. Civil War historians are far too willing to concede the field to foreign evaluations in this regard. Although their motives are clearly suspect, the estimates of Confederate partisan-historians are much closer to the mark: the South, like Brandenburg-Prussia, nurtured soldiers of outstanding competence, Lee being only the most famous.[1]

Napoleon and Wellington were extremely lucky in their adversaries: until his final confrontation with Wellington, the only first-rate general the Corsican had to fight was Archduke Charles. None of Wellington's peninsular opponents were any better than the Austrian Mack or the Prussian Blücher, and most of them were considerably worse. A single example suffices: at Waterloo Napoleon's army simply dissolved when the final charges failed. At Shiloh, Beauregard managed the most difficult of operations, a successful retreat in the face of a victorious enemy.

Genius is difficult to describe, and impossible to explain, but one measure of just how good Grant was is to be found in an objective consideration of his opponents, by and large world-class commanders whose troops would have made short work of any British or European adversary.

This judgment is hotly denied; there is a veritable cottage industry in Great Britain denigrating the competence and combat effectiveness of the nineteenth-century American military. Again, a single example punctures the delusion. In January 1815, a greatly outnumbered American force, hastily cobbled together by Andrew Jackson, clashed with 10,000 British veterans of Wellington's peninsular campaigns, led by his brother-in-law, Pakenham. Outnumbered by at least two to one, the Americans simply annihilated their British opponents in the last battle ever fought between the two Atlantic powers; the casualty exchange ratio was roughly fifty to one.

Although it is customary to see Grant as a bumpkin who learned warfare and leadership quickly, this is hardly the case. Like these other famous generals, he simply had an instinct for his profession. There was no learning curve. His only weakness was a certain naivete about his fellow human beings, the one area where Napoleon was clearly superior, albeit at a certain moral cost.

There are three main reasons for Grant's success. The key to the first may be found in his flirtation with painting and drawing. Grant could look out over the terrain and visualize it perfectly, and he could do the same with the rather crude maps of his day. He apparently carried around in his head a three dimensional map of the battlefield, and always used the terrain to his advantage. Today's army, having developed the most advanced technology in this field, refining tools such as radars, night vision, and satellite images, has clearly continued to consider the accurate knowledge of terrain a central role in preparation for warfare.

The second key is to be found in Grant's encyclopedic knowledge of military history, a knowledge uncontaminated by any obsession with the military theories that disfigured warfare after 1815. As the French general Phillipe Pétain put it, "In war nothing is more dangerous than theorists."[2] Or, as Grant himself put it, "if men make war in slavish observances of the rules, they will fail."[3] The bizarre ideas of Henry Halleck are an excellent argument for the truth of the assertion.

Grant however derived the basic underlying principles that were the preconditions for success rather than preconceived rules: speed, aggression, and keeping one's attention fixed on the main objectives. Our military leaders all receive a solid education in military history when they train to be soldiers and learn to apply leadership styles and lessons learned from their predecessors, knowing how to adapt them, as Grant did, and taking into account the changes brought about by advances in technology and the ever-changing nature of the enemy.

The third key to Grant's genius is more remarked: the clear and unambiguous quality of his written orders. Here is a brief extract of his initial order to Sherman to proceed on Vicksburg.

> You will proceed, with as little delay as possible, to Memphis, Tennessee, taking with you one division of your present command. On your arrival at Memphis, you will assume command of all troops there. . . . As soon as possible, move with them down the river to the vicinity of Vicksburg, and with the co-operation of the gunboat fleet under the command of Flag-office Porter proceed to the reduction of that place in such manner as circumstances, and your own judgment, may dictate. . . . [4]

As armies become larger, and forces are dispersed over wider areas—and often far away from central command—clear written orders are essential. Grant's style of communication, efficient, succinct, and consistent, has become of extreme importance.

One reason Grant was able to make an easy transition from a field commander to general in chief was that this habit was already ingrained: it made little difference to him whether the order was carried by a staff officer over the hill or sent by telegram a thousand miles.

So too in his speech; Grant kept his own counsel, partly owing to the fact that Northern newspapers printed military secrets wholesale, but his occasional remarks have all the force of Napoleon's maxims: "The only way to whip an army is to go out and fight it," he remarked.[5] And, unlike

Napoleon, whose celebrated maxims are often contradictory (and who was not above rewriting history to his own advantage), Grant's were consistent, and resonated with what had actually taken place.

<hr/>

Grant's victories were not achieved through sheer application of brute force. The noted British military historian J. F. C. Fuller rather thoroughly debunked the notion of Grant as a crude butcher back in the 1920s, and no one who has looked at the casualty figures can come to any other conclusion, although for some reason the notion has remarkable persistence.[6] In fact, it would be closer to the truth to turn the idea around: one reason for the eventual failure of Confederate arms was the wastage of manpower. The South simply could not afford to lose men at the rate it did. Victories in which the losses on both sides were roughly equal were essentially meaningless triumphs; for the South probably the only occasion where they were justified was at Shiloh.

Grant's genius was essentially strategic: he saw how to win the war and stuck to his objectives. It was hardly his fault that his superiors continuously wandered off course, prolonging the conflict for years. But this is not to suggest that he was tactically deficient, although it must be said that entirely too much weight has been placed on tactical innovation as a marker of great generalship.

Frederick the Great introduced tactical innovations to the battlefield. Napoleon, despite claims to the contrary, did not. Wellington noted his surprise after Waterloo: "Napoleon did not maneuver at all. He just moved forward in the old style, in columns, and was driven off in the old style. The only difference was, that he mixed cavalry with infantry, and supported both with an enormous quantity of artillery."[7]

The rifled musket forced changes in battlefield tactics, and the impact of these can be seen from Grant's order to the advancing divisions at Shiloh to form heavy skirmish lines well in advance of the main force. The preferred Prussian tactic of flank attacks was well known to both sides, but there were times and places where this approach was impracticable. Grant attempted to put his opponents into a position where their only options were to surrender or be killed, thus minimizing the death toll as much as was possible.

Although extensive studies have been done on the evolution of tactics during the war, the matter is somewhat over-stated: head-on frontal attacks were fewer than is commonly supposed, and most of them were in situations where there was no alternative, once the enemy showed a willingness to fight. The generals of the Civil War were basically much more sophisticated than their British and French counterparts in the First World War, who really did hurl masses of infantry at entrenched positions without any regard for loss. Nor were frontal attacks limited to these early wars: as American commanders were sadly aware in the Second World War, sometimes there was no other alternative, particularly when it came to amphibious landings.

The key—where true genius came to bear—was in knowing when frontal assaults were necessary and when they were delusional. As we have seen, on the few occasions where Grant ordered direct assaults, he regretted them afterwards; but generally investigation shows that the losses were caused by the vanity of the actual unit commanders, and were not a result of Grant's directives.

Tactically, Grant's great achievement was his reorganization and deployment of the cavalry, whose use had languished as the rifled musket came into use. Grant took all the cavalry units and merged them into one; typically, he then passed over the horse officers and picked a young infantry commander for the job: Major General Phillip Sheridan, which suggests Grant was a pretty good talent spotter. By 1900, Grant's idea of how cavalry should be used (primarily for screening and reconnaissance) was standard procedure in the great European armies (although not the British).

His other emphasis was on speed. He took Napoleon's maxim and pushed it much further than Napoleon did. Speed is the basis for all tactical moves, and many strategic ones. German success in two world wars was not, as is often thought, a function of new and better weapons, or of some new tactic, it was a function of being able to move faster than their opponents. Grant's repeated exhortations to Thomas in December 1864 strike right to the heart of the matter, and of the three military historians who have looked at Grant's generalship in detail, there is certainly a consensus about his achievements in that area and the importance of the concept itself.[8]

✛━━━✛

Where Grant truly excelled was in his understanding of the troops under his command. They were of quite a different sort from those of the prewar army, where in general soldiers were soldiers because they were unfit for any honest work. The men on both sides of the Civil War were a reasonable cross section of society, civilians who had put on a uniform. They had to be treated accordingly, and Grant's modesty, his disregard for pomp and brass, stood him in good stead, even though it was not an act. Lee entered the war already a legend, but Grant became one owing to his generalship. As Lee himself put it: "I have carefully searched the military records of both ancient and modern history, and have never found Grant's superior as a general."[9]

Mention of the great Southern general of course invites the obvious comparison. By the time the two were sparring in Virginia, Grant was responsible for every Union army in the field, while Lee was only responsible for the Army of Northern Virginia. Not only did Grant have more on his plate, but, realizing he could not direct all the armies and run one himself, he had to transmit his orders through others. The situation with Meade, the supposed victor of Gettysburg, was particularly sensitive, and not helped by Meade's temper, intelligence, and personality. Or, to look at it another way, one reason Grant was so successful as overall commander was that he was able to delegate authority.

Lee's style of leadership was perfectly suited to the size of his command, and to the fact that he was not the leader of all the Confederate forces in the field, but simply the first among his equals. Moreover, after Chattanooga, Lincoln, seeing in Grant the first competent general he had found in the army, stepped back and let him run the war. From that point on, Lincoln became the perfect model for a wartime president.

Jefferson Davis, by contrast, drew on his West Point education and military service to the extent that it often seems he was micromanaging his generals, and anyone who reads Lee's correspondence with Davis is struck by how deferential Lee is. Whether Davis was a good president for the Confederacy or not, he was determined to manage the strategy of the war, the result being that the Confederacy squandered its brainpower in more or less the same fashion that France would do in the First World War, losing as many French soldiers in combat on the Western Front as the Germans did on all three fronts.[10]

Lee's generalship was impressive testimony to the vitality of a military tradition in the United States; Grant's was proof that the country could produce a military genius.

+>==<+

Military genius is particularly difficult to describe in Grant's case because of the peculiar nature of the Civil War. Both sides had to raise armies from civilians, without any existing framework to guide them. Moreover, the Civil War was the last war in which commanding generals could personally direct the course of the battle.

These two factors, when taken together, make Grant unique. The great European and British generals who came before him all commanded armies with illustrious traditions: Wellington led the British army to victory, but it had existed as a significant professional fighting force long before he was born. And although many of the talented generals after Grant also commanded masses of civilians in uniforms, they all had trained staffs as well as professional cadres of officers.

But many aspects of Grant's genius can still be divined in the American military, and may fairly be said to constitute his greatest legacy. The first of these deserves special note. Grant was not the sort of man who tried to browbeat people by parading his superior knowledge of military history, or by intimidating others with some abstruse theory of warfare.

His knowledge of both bordered on encyclopedic. To paraphrase one of Teddy Roosevelt's memorable remarks, Grant walked softly but he carried a formidable intellectual stick. It is no accident that after Grant, American officers became some of the most highly educated and intellectually proficient warriors in the world. That this is often a little noted fact is also part of Grant's legacy.

The other aspects of Grant's genius that have had a lasting impact are directly relevant to battlefield command. Unlike most of his contemporaries, Grant understood the common soldier. It was an instinctive grasp of the hopes and needs of his fellow Americans, not something done for show. The only two great generals in the twentieth century who had demonstrated a similar empathy for their soldiers are the British general Bernard Montgomery and the French general Phillipe Pétain.

In Grant's time it was extremely difficult to show that kind of leadership; that he made it look easy does not mean that it was so. Nowadays, in an age when all soldiers are volunteers, and often specialists of a very high order, the task is much easier than formerly: one specialist understands another, regardless of rank.

We therefore take it for granted that officers respect the men in their command, and feel a moral responsibility to look after them. As one weary infantry captain said, standing on the tarmac of Charles de Gaulle airport, "I have to go back to Baghdad. My men need me."[11] That sentiment is part of Grant's legacy.

This understanding, or empathy, goes hand in hand with another notable skill: Grant was able to depend on his soldiers because he made it clear that he had a very high opinion of them. They became as good as they were because he behaved as though they were as good as he claimed. In his comments after the war, he repeatedly spoke of the Union army as the best army in the world. It is to Grant that the army owes the sort of confidence exhibited by an American officer's retort to a worried and distraught French officer in June 1918: "General, these are American regulars. In a hundred and fifty years they have never been beaten."[12]

Grant's quiet confidence and his unassuming mask of command have set a very high standard for his successors. The most important part of Grant's significance as a military leader, the lesson he has for us today, is his attitude, his calm steadiness, together with his unwavering confidence in his men, and this has become an example for American officers. Although often unremarked, it has become what we might call the signature of the American commander. The American military of today is very much the army of Ulysses S. Grant.

CHAPTER 13

The Undervalued President

ALTHOUGH GEORGE WASHINGTON AND ANDREW JACKSON had both been generals, neither one thought of himself as a professional army officer, or had envisioned the army as a career. Zachary Taylor was the country's first professional soldier to be elected president. But Taylor's case is so complicated, so unique, that we can draw very little from it. When Taylor entered office in 1849, he was sixty-five and in poor health. He had barely moved into the White House before he was taken ill and died. As we shall see below, there was one clear link to Taylor in Grant's handling of the office, but basically Taylor was not president long enough for us to have any idea of what the relationship between military command and the presidency might be.

Properly seen, then, Grant was the first professional soldier to become president; Dwight D. Eisenhower was the only other soldier to achieve this office in our nation's history. So Grant's presidency, although technically outside the scope of any evaluation of his achievements as general, provides us with an interesting glimpse into the difficulties of transition from military to civilian leadership. Can we discern any ways in which his background and achievements as a general had some significant bearing on how he approached the problems of the presidency?

Unfortunately, most Americans do not have much of an awareness of what happened during Grant's two terms as president, or even the circumstances of his election. Briefly put, the situation was this: Abraham Lincoln, who had been elected as a Republican in 1860, had defeated the incumbent president, the Democrat James Buchanan (elected in 1856). Lincoln won re-election, and was then murdered. He was succeeded by his vice-president, Andrew Johnson, who, as the result of a series of confrontations with Congress, was impeached. The attempt failed, but Johnson was decisively beaten at the polls by Grant, who then became the first president since Andrew Jackson (1829–1837) to serve two full terms.

Grant was one of the relatively few American presidents up to that time to be re-elected. In the first century of our existence, there were nineteen presidents, and only seven of them were re-elected to a second term: George Washington, Thomas Jefferson, James Madison, James Monroe, Andrew Jackson, Abraham Lincoln, and Ulysses Grant. After Grant left office in 1877, nearly a quarter of a century would pass before another American president would serve two successive terms (Theodore Roosevelt, elected in 1901).

So the mere fact of re-election is an accomplishment; one moreover that puts Grant in very select company, as our list makes clear. Consequently Grant has been judged against the likes of Washington and Jefferson, somewhat to his detriment, since probably the only concrete notion most people have of his presidency is that it was racked by scandal and corruption.

The ranking of presidents is a curious business, and more or less analogous to the one by which commanders like Henry Halleck are scrubbed for virtues and their point of view treated as though deserving of serious merit. A practical example: when Arthur Schlesinger told John F. Kennedy how highly his profession rated Woodrow Wilson, Kennedy, who knew his American history, was incredulous. In recent years, Wilson's star has begun to tarnish, and there has been a slight improvement in the assessment of Grant, although he remains perhaps our most undervalued president.[1]

+>━<+

Grant had a somewhat unique problem: almost universally hailed by Americans in 1870 as our country's greatest general, his military reputation inevitably eclipsed his presidency. Some of this was Grant's fault. As we have seen, he was unassuming and reserved, not the sort of man who engaged in self-aggrandizement. In his memoirs, justly acknowledged as being one of the great personal experience narratives of American literature, Grant gave short shrift to his two terms in office as President of the United States. When, after he left the office and traveled the world, it was as General Grant, not as President Grant.

It is also quite true that there were numerous scandals during his presidency, and these may easily be traced to the one serious defect of character we have already noted, an all too trusting belief in the goodness of his fellow men.

This leads us to a consideration of the extent to which Grant's military life did not prepare him for a political life. Although, as we have seen, Grant was saddled with a goodly share of problem generals, many of them political appointees, in the main, the military leadership in the Civil War consisted almost exclusively of men who had been trained as professional soldiers. A fact often cited is worth repeating: of the sixty major engagements of the war, West Point graduates commanded both sides in fifty-five, and one side in the other five.

Although their battlefield performance varied widely, it must be said that these West Point graduates were men who possessed in great measure the virtues we would wish our generals to possess. They were not merely courageous, they were moral. By contrast with the political and business classes of the time, one could almost see them as saintly. This is not a distinction that can be pushed very far, but it is very much at the root of the troubles Grant had as president.

It is often said that the problem generals have in political office is that in the military everyone does what he's told, and in civilian life, they don't.

Whether this is true or not, it certainly was not true in Grant's day. In recounting Grant's battles and campaigns, we have seen numerous examples of subordinates who didn't follow orders, or deliberately went off and did something else entirely.

But even in the worst of these cases, the officer concerned was motivated not by greed but by the desire to win military fame. Henry Halleck may well have been the best general the Confederacy possessed. Two of the twentieth century's most distinguished military historians argue for this. But by all the available evidence, he genuinely believed he was doing the right thing, he did pretty much what Lincoln told him to do, and he certainly didn't take advantage of his position to fill his pockets.

✦━━✦

To put it bluntly: Grant's experiences as a soldier did not prepare him to deal with the deceit, the shameless self-interest, and the sometimes legally questionable machinations of the people who often surround presidents. All of this was exacerbated by the lack of most of the safeguards against corruption and scandal that were eventually put in place. In the 1870s, the government of the United States managed its affairs in a way that was much closer to the way British affairs had been handled a century before, when bribery and patronage were simply assumed as the entitlements of office.

Although in the popular mind the scandals have tended to eclipse everything else, resulting in a vaguely negative aura surrounding the Grant presidency, his actual achievements were impressive, and provide us with an interesting lesson in the relevance of military command experience to the presidency.

Grant clearly understood the importance of being seen to be in command, something he had observed with Zachary Taylor. Indeed, this is the one clear link between the two men, and allows us a glimpse into how the military shaped their views of the office.

Although Taylor was a Southerner and a slave owner, he saw the United States as a national entity, and faced down the talk of secession that was leading the nation to a crisis point in 1850. He did so in explicit military terms, assuring his fellow Southerners that he would not only take personal command of an army to defeat them, but treat them just as he had treated deserters and petty thieves in the military, that is, by promptly hanging them from the nearest tree.

Whatever his personal views, Taylor spoke as the president of the whole country, as a man who was immune to the desires of one particular political party or faction. So did Grant. Both men's view of the office was thus parallel to their role as general. Generals are not elected, but once in the field, they represent the national interest at a very practical level.

+>——+——<+

Although as time passed there has been a tendency to see Grant as controlled by various factions, this is simply part and parcel of the same attempt to credit others with his military victories, or to see him as a wasteful butcher. At the time, Grant was very much seen to be running things. In fact he was hotly criticized for not doing more, a fact that suggests how successful he was in establishing a presidential presence. Conceptually, psychologically, Grant approached the job as he had approached the job of being a military commander. He made the decisions, took the responsibility for what happened, and was seen to do so. We can see this quite clearly in the two major challenges of his presidency.

Grant's greatest accomplishment in office was his handling of the financial disasters of the collapse of 1873. Grant was severely pressured to solve the rather complex technical problem by simply issuing more money, and in April 1874, Congress passed a bill mandating just that, assuming that he would bow to the overwhelming pressure and sign it. As every economist understands, printing more money is a ruinous solution that only makes things much worse. What Congress and much of the population were asking for was a ticket to national disaster.

As a general, Grant had kept his own counsel, made his own decisions, ignoring the doubts and fears of his subordinates as well as of his superiors. He held no councils of war, explaining afterwards that he felt that the divisions of opinion only hardened once they were expressed. As we have seen, it is very clear that his command decisions were his, not someone else's.

He applied the same approach to the presidency. Economic issues were new to him, and complex. But he studied the matter carefully, and then, to everyone's amazement and consternation, he vetoed the bill, and the veto was sustained. Although economics is far too complex an issue for any one act to be crucial, there's little doubt in retrospect that the bill was ill-advised, and that Grant was quite right in his rejection of it.

In so doing, he demonstrated real leadership of the same sort that he showed as a general. He was as unmoved by the fears of politicians as he had previously been by the fears of his subordinates. Once he saw what he believed to be in the national interest, he was not willing to make any sort of political compromise. In this he differed sharply from Lincoln, who was more than willing to tack in a different direction if he thought it politically expedient. In fall 1861, for example, he fired General John Frémont for emancipating slaves in his Missouri command, only to issue his own proclamation later on. Given the nature of the war, Lincoln may well have been right, and his decision has generally been seen favorably by historians, but it was also very clearly a political move of the sort that a man makes with an eye to maintaining himself in office. There was an element of calculation in it that is quite absent in Grant.

Grant also provided the nation with a steady and focused leader during one of the most difficult periods in our national history, his second major achievement. When Andrew Johnson, the vice-president, assumed the presidency after the assassination of Lincoln, he promptly became entangled in a series of controversies with Congress over what is called "Reconstruction," the thorny question of how to rebuild Southern society politically, morally, and economically.

The struggle led to his impeachment. Although it failed, the struggle polarized an already deeply divided nation. The resulting wounds, constantly reopened by fanatics and bigots of all sorts, took years to heal. They were beyond the power of any man, any president, to resolve in eight short years. But what Grant did do as president was to enforce the Fourteenth and Fifteenth Amendments, which, taken together, ensured that the newly freed slaves would have the right to vote. Under his prodding, Congress authorized the creation of a Department of Justice to ensure that these two amendments were enforced.

This stand was much more difficult than it seems in retrospect. Several Northern states had withdrawn their ratifications of the amendments, and the whole issue of universal suffrage was much more problematic than we think of it as being today. Again, Grant did what he believed to be in the national interest, and, again, history has proven him right. It is to Grant that we owe the institutionalization of the universal suffrage and racial equality that we take for granted today.

+━━━+

Unlike many presidents before and after him, Grant was not only re-elected, but he won decisively. But even during his lifetime, he was known and appreciated more for his military accomplishments than the presidency. The achievements of his two terms were overshadowed by his achievements on the battlefield, and that remains the case today.

Had Grant not been so great a general, his historical ranking as a president would probably have been higher. Of the four successful American generals who became presidents (Jackson, Eisenhower, and Taylor being the others), Grant achieved the most in both areas. To anyone familiar with the period, that is high praise indeed. It is well deserved. It is difficult to think of any American who rendered his country greater service than Ulysses S. Grant.

Notes

Chapter 1 Notes

1. The subtitle of Brooks D. Simpson's *Grant: Triumph Over Adversity, 1822–1865* (New York: Houghton Mifflin, 200). A good illustration of how little we know about Grant's early life: of the over 500 pages Simpson devotes to this period of Grant's life, only 77 are devoted to the period before April 1861—about the same proportion as in the other, major, biographies.
2. Josiah Bunting III, *Ulysses S. Grant* (New York: Henry Holt, 2004) 2.
3. Nigel Hamilton, *Monty: The Making of A General, 187–1942* (New York: Mc-Graw Hill, 1981), 438.
4. Robert Parker in *Memoirs of the Most Remarkable Transactions from 1683 to 1718* (London, 1847), as quoted by David Chandler, *Marlborough as Military Commander* (New York: Charles Scribner's Sons, 1973), 1.
5. Three typical paintings are at www.mscomm.com/~ulysses/page154.html.

Chapter 2 Notes

1. Ulysses S. Grant, *The Personal Memoirs of U. S. Grant,* edited E. B. Long (New York: Da Capo Press, 1982), 24.
2. "The cost in American lives was staggering. Of the 104,556 men who served in the army, both regulars and volunteers, 13,768 men died. It was the highest death rate of any war in our history, according to John D. Eisenhower, citing evidence in Major General Emery Upton, *The Military Policy of the United* States (Washington, D. C.: Government Printing Office, 1917 [1881]), 216–218. The quote and source are in Eisenhower, *So Far From God: The U. S. War with Mexico, 1846–1848* (New York: Random House, 1989), xviii. This data is different from current Department of Defense figures, but the basic contention still stands. See the discussion

in Jean Edward Smith, *Grant* (New York: Simon and Schuster, 2001) 36, 631.

3. In *Ulysses S. Grant: Triumph Over Adversity, 1822–1865* (New York: Houghton Mifflin, 2000), Brooks D. Simpson, author of most authoritative account of Grant's life, discusses the issue, implying the same conclusion (pages 60–62). Geoffrey Perret points out the unusual number of resignations, and emphasizes that Grant hung on so he could resign as a captain, rather than as a lieutenant. See his excellent *Ulysses S. Grant* (New York: Random House, 1997) 100–102.

4. It is one of the pillars of what the distinguished presidential historian Josiah Bunting calls "the clichés of the Grant Myth." (*Ulysses S. Grant,* 3). The other cliché, that Grant was simply a butcher, has been thoroughly debunked by military historians, as will become clear in the chapters that follow.

5. The diagnostic first used by clinicians, and enshrined in the 1952 edition of the *Diagnostic and Statistical Manual of Mental Disorders* (DSM I-II), broke down alcoholics into three specific categories: episodic, habitual, and addictive. The criteria for the first two were purely quantitative: episodic meant the person was intoxicated more than four times a year, habitual meant twelve times a year or once a week, and addictive meant the person had to drink daily. In the 1970s, more research was done on this subject, resulting in a more sophisticated standard, the one currently embodied in DSM-IV and in the guidelines of the National Institute on Alcohol Abuse and Alcoholism.

   This standard is less quantitative, and places more emphasis on consequent adverse behaviors that would annually, such as the inability to perform at work, states of intoxication putting the drinker in physical danger, recurrent legal problems resulting from drinking, and impairment of personal relationships. Using the newer standard, as embodied by DSM-IV, it is highly doubtful that Grant can be diagnosed even as a case of alcohol abuse. See the extensive discussion in Marc A. Schuckit, Peter E. Nathan, John E. Helzer, George E. Woody, Tom J. Crowley "Evolution of the DSM diagnostic criteria for alcoholism—Diagnostic and Statistical Manual of Mental Disorders," *Alcohol Health & Research World* (Fall, 1991), at www.findarticles.com/p/articles/mi_m0847/is_n4_v15/ai_12754641.

6. Ellen Thackerey and Madeline Harris, editors, *The Gale Encyclopedia of Mental Disorders* (Detroit, Michigan: Gale Group, 2003) 1.34

7. The house still stands. See the picture of it in William S. McFeely, *Ulysses S. Grant, An Album* (New York: W. W. Norton, 2004), 92. As McFeely notes, it was "a comfortable house."

Chapter 3 Notes

1. As recounted by William Wellington Greener, *The Gun and Its Development,* 9th edition. (London, Cassell and Company, 1910), 740. Greener has numer-

ous other examples. In the Crimean War, the French fired 25 million cartridges; it is doubtful even 25,000 Russian soldiers were hit (740).

2. Secretary of War, *Report of the Surgeon General for 1920* (w1.1:920/1): 49. In this sense the Civil War was a modern war. French medical services recorded casualties from edged weapons at roughly one third of one percent. See Michel Huber, *La population de la France pendant la guerre* (New Haven: Yale University Press, 1931), 431. The German medical services went one step further and didn't even bother to record these cases.

3. Extensive data on the accuracy of rifled muskets can be found in Greener, *The Gun and Its Development*, 633. "Provided an American rifleman was to get a perfect aim at 300 yards at me standing still, he most undoubtedly would hit me, unless it was a very windy day," Colonel Hanger observed. As quoted by Peter Newark, *Firefight: The History of Personal Firepower* (Devon: David and Charles, 1988), 27. See also the extensive discussions, citing different experiments, in Brent Nosworthy, *The Bloody Crucible of Courage* (New York: Carrol and Graf, 2003), 22–39.

4. The best estimate is that the rate of fire increased roughly by half, thanks to development in cartridges such as the Minié and the Greener. Once armies went to breechloaders, the increase in rate of fire was dramatic. Sturdy, reliable, breech loading rifles were introduced in small numbers during the last years of the Civil War, the notable examples being the Henry and the Spencer. Although used by Union troops, only about 200,000 Spencers, and less than 15,000 Henry rifles were made. Production data is found in Claud E. Fuller, *The Rifled Musket* (Harrisburg, Pennsylvania, 1958) 1. The title is misleading: the book contains technical data as well as production and test information for all major rifles and muskets used in the Civil War

5. As John Keegan points out, speaking of Shiloh, "It was a tract of territory, indeed, on which no European army would ever have offered or given battle. . . . It was an entirely American landscape, one of those wildernesses which settlement as yet had scarcely touched," *The Mask of Command* (New York: Viking, 1987) 167. What Keegan neglects to say is that this same description was true of almost the entire region, excepting a few portions of Virginia and Maryland.

6. Horace Porter, *Campaigning with Grant*, edited Wayne C. Temple (New York: Bonanza Books, 1961), 373. "Whipped" was a favorite Grant word.

7. For the exact quotation, see Gerhard Ritter, *Der Schlieffenplan: Kritik eines Mythos* (München: Oldenbourg, 1956) 54.

8. Casualty data for this and other engagements taken from Thomas L. Livermore, *Numbers and Losses in the Civil War in America* (Bloomington, Indiana: University of Indiana Press, 1957), 102–103. This study was first published in 1900. It is universally agreed that the casualties at Gettysburg were the worst of the war: 17,684 Union killed and wounded, and 22,638 Confederate. There are higher figures, but these count the missing in action.

Livermore, a combat veteran, excluded these from his totals, as he felt they were simply men who were lost, and would eventually return to their units. This is probably true. It was only in the First World War that the word "missing" began to have the horrific connotations which it now carries: "missing, presumed dead," a euphemism for "we can't find what's left of him." Thus we assume that most of the 45,899 British soldiers officially listed as missing for the Battle of the Somme were mostly dead, and should be added to the total of 108,724 killed. See the figures in War Office [United Kingdom], *Statistics of the Military Effort of the British Empire During the Great War, 1914–1920* (London: His Majesty's Stationery Office, 1922), 324.

9. After the First World War, shrapnel became a generic term used to indicate shell fragments, because the standard shell used quickly became a shell containing an explosive charge. Before 1914, however, shrapnel shells were standard issue for artillery. Think of them as spherical shotgun shells: when fired, the casing ruptures and spews out a stream of small metal pellets. It was several years into the war before the British gunners realized that shrapnel shells would not cut barbed wire. Historically, shrapnel came in three different varieties. The differences were mostly in the size of the individual balls in the shell, and how they were packed. The oldest, called Grape Shot, had been designed for naval cannon. The shot was bagged, and took time to rupture and release the pellets. In Canister, the pellets were released when the shell left the muzzle—technically, this was the only kind of shrapnel that was precisely analogous to a shotgun blast. For the British, the true shrapnel shell was a projectile invented by the British gunner, Henry Shrapnel. Everyone else called it Case Shot. Shrapnel's idea was to embed the shot in solid mass that would quickly melt and disperse as an air burst. This required a time delay fuse. Air bursts were theoretically devastating to troops in open ground, but the time delay mechanisms (fuses) were expensive and delicate. Even in the First World War, most shells fired had the basic percussion fuse.

10. Rifled guns were categorized by the diameter of the gun tube as opposed to the weight of the shell, since increasingly they fired explosive shells, making the weight was irrelevant—except in the British Army, which was still using the antique designations all through the Second World War. In modern parlance, we should say that Parrott's first gun, the 10-pounder, was a 2.9 inch weapon, as opposed to the 3 inch weapon that became the standard field gun: both the French 75 millimeter and the German 7.7 centimeter field guns of 1914 were roughly three inches. After the First World War, the American army went metric, the British stuck with their eighteenth century classifications, and the Germans insisted on using centimeters rather than meters: the corresponding German tank gun was known as a 7.5 centimeter weapon.

11. The enlistments problem, which directly determines the actual numbers of men in uniform during the war, is a difficult matter to solve. It occupies Thomas Livermore for most of *Numbers and Losses in the Civil War in Amer-*

ica (Bloomington, Indiana: University of Indiana Press, 1957), and it takes him 63 pages of dense statistical reasoning to work up his conclusion, which is this: the number of actual soldiers enlisted (as distinct from the number of enlistments) is 1,556,678 Union soldiers and 1,082,119 Confederate soldiers. There are other ways of computing the troop strengths, giving a considerably higher number for the Union, but the same ratio still holds.

Chapter 4 Notes

1. Wilson's Creek is one of those minor skirmishes no one talks about. Russell F. Weigley, in his fine history of the war, *A Great Civil War* (Bloomington, Indiana: University of Indiana Press, 2000), devotes one sentence to it (page 87). In *The Battle Cry of Freedom* (New York: Oxford University Press, 1988) James McPherson has a brief discussion and gives slightly different figures (pages 351–352). The differences reflect differing estimates of Confederate losses. According to Thomas Livermore in *Numbers and Losses in the Civil War in America* (Bloomington, Indiana: University of Indiana Press, 1957), 78, the Union troops, outnumbered 11,600 to 5,400, lost 1,235 (223 killed, 721 wounded, 291 missing) while inflicting on the Confederates a loss of 1,184 (257 killed, 900 wounded, 27 missing). In the other comprehensive accounting of casualties, Frederick Phisterer gives the same Union figures, but lumping Confederate losses together, lists them at 1,094. See his *Statistical Record of the Armies of the United States* (New York: Charles Scribner's Sons, 1883), 213.

2. *Harper's Monthly,* September and December 1861. Studies of the First Bull Run introduce a novel concept into military history: special pleading for the loser, in this case General MacDowell, who, it is alleged, was badly served by his subordinate officers. Had it not been for that, the argument goes, the Union might very well have won. This is rubbish: any battle can be deconstructed so as to suggest that the loser might have won. When an officer commands one side in a battle, the only test of competency is victory. Battles measure battlefield success, not the intentions, intelligence, or personality of the commanders.

3. Robert M. Johnston, *Bull Run: Its Strategy and Tactics* (Carlisle, Pennsylvania: John Kallman, 1996 [1910]) 125. This study is very ancient, but in many respects still unsurpassed. In *A Great Civil War,* Weigley spins the battle neatly enough, arguing that it wasn't really much of a Union defeat (62–63). This is to miss the point: it was widely believed to be one at the time.

4. For comments in Wellington's correspondence, see *Dispatches of Field-Marshal the Duke of Wellington,* edited Walter Wood (London: Grant and Richards, 1902), especially 189, 202. This quote taken from in Elizabeth Longford, *Wellington, The Years of the Sword* (New York: Harper and Row, 1969), 420.

5. Although Fort Heiman is never mentioned in accounts of Grant's early campaign, it still exists, and it was very much a factor in the attack—as we shall

see below, Grant allocated the investment of that fort to his most experienced commander, Charles F. Smith.

6. Gideon Welles, as quoted—disapprovingly, by the anonymous author in the brief biography at www.civilwarhome.com/halleckbio.htm. The ultimate source is Stephen Ambrose, who challenged the conventional interpretation of the general in *Halleck: Lincoln's Chief of Staff* (Baron Rouge, Louisiana: Louisiana State University Press, 1996). This is a prime example of the remaking of bad generals. Like any competent peacetime officer, Halleck had certain virtues, which Ambrose adumbrates. As a wartime commander, none of them were very helpful.

7. Troop Strengths taken from Thomas L. Livermore, *Numbers and Losses in the Civil War in America* (Bloomington, Indiana: University of Indiana Press, 1957), 77.

8. A well known passage, taken from Lew Wallace, "The Capture of Fort Donelson," in *Battles and Leaders of the Civil War,* edited Ned Bradford (New York: Dutton, 1956) 422. Partially quoted in McPherson, *Battle Cry,* 401.

9. As quoted by General André Beaufre (who was present at the time), in *The Fall of France,* translated Desmond Flower (New York: Knopf, 1968), 182.

10. In terms of losses, Donelson was the tenth bloodiest battle of the Civil War. Data taken from Thomas L. Livermore, *Numbers and Losses in the Civil War in America* (Bloomington, Indiana: University of Indiana Press, 1957), 78. Curiously, the battle gets short shrift by contemporary writers.

11. As quoted by Owen Connelly, *Blundering To Glory: Napoleon's Military Campaigns* (Wilmington, Delaware: Scholarly Resources, 1987), 90.

Chapter 5 Notes

1. Field Marshall Heinrich Hess, as quoted by Geoffrey Wawro, *The Franco-Prussian War* (Cambridge: Cambridge University Press, 2003), 47.

2. It is customary to posit an opposition here: on the one hand, learned military theorists like Halleck and Buell, on the other, the unschooled Grant. This opposition paints Grant as a sort of idiot savant: ignorant of theory, he learned from experience and his own mistakes. But he didn't understand the principles that Buell and Halleck were applying, the theory from which they were derived. These ideas are usually tracked back to Jomini, supposedly the dominant military historian and theorist of the age. Halleck's whole claim to intellectual fame was his redaction and translation of Jomini on Napoleon. The idea of the importance of Jomini and theory to Civil War generals may probably be traced back to T. Harry Williams' seminal essay, "The Military Leadership of the North and South," in *Why the North Won the Civil War* (New York: Simon and Schuster, 1960), 42–46. And, as John Keegan points out, Grant's knowledge of military history was encyclopedic. See his examples in *The Mask of Command* (New York: Viking, 1987), 213.

3. As reported by John Russell Young, Around *the World with General Grant*, edited Michael Fellman (Baltimore: Johns Hopkins University Press, 2002), 158.
4. *Harper's Weekly*, January 17, 1863: 34.
5. For a succinct guide to the confusing nomenclature employed by the Union Army, see Frederick Phisterer, *Statistical Record of the Armies of the United States* (New York: Charles Scribner's Sons, 1883), 51–53.
6. For a fuller discussion of McClellan's alleged instability and Halleck's role in the intrigues against him, see Thomas J. Rowland, *George McClellan and Civil War History* (Kent, Ohio: Kent State University, 1998), especially ix-x.

Chapter 6 Notes

1. Extract from a dispatch reprinted in its entirety in William T. Sherman, *Memoirs of General W. T. Sherman* (New York: Library of America, 1990), 176.
2. A famous quote. In this form taken from J. F. C. Fuller, *The Generalship of Ulysses S. Grant* (New York: Da Capo Press, 1991), 110.
3. As quoted by Jay Luvaas, *Napoleon on the Art of War* (New York: Simon and Schuster, 1999) 60.
4. Figures taken from Thomas L. Livermore, *Numbers and Losses in the Civil War in America* (Bloomington: University of Indiana Press, 1957), 79–80. The data may be spun by counting the missing. As mentioned above, Livermore, who was a combat veteran of the war, listed the missing but excluded them from his casualty totals. Figures for prisoners and the missing are rarely given for other nineteenth-century wars.
5. Ulysses S. Grant, *The Personal Memoirs of U. S. Grant*, edited E. B. Long (New York: Da Capo Press, 1982), 191.

Chapter 7 Notes

1. January 17, 1863: 34.
2. There is a succinct account of the newspapers' role in smearing Grant in Simpson, *Ulysses S. Grant*, 137–138. Simpson's characterization of one reporter's accounts could stand for the whole: "reports more notable for their color and drama than for their accuracy," but this understates the matter considerably (137). See also the extensive account of how the press covered the war in J. Cutler Adams, *The North Reports the Civil War* (Pittsburgh, PA: University of Pittsburgh Press, 1955).
3. For a cogent analysis of the modern situation, see William V. Kennedy, *The Military and the Media: Why the Press Cannot Be Trusted to Cover a War* (New York: Praeger, 1993).
4. Ulysses S. Grant, *The Personal Memoirs of U. S. Grant*, edited E. B. Long (New York: Da Capo Press, 1982), 373.
5. Wellington, like Frederick the Great, had a surprisingly laid-back view of such things, as did Grant, who observed that men who ran away would generally

return to the fight. Quote from Elizabeth Longford, *Wellington, The Years of the Sword* (New York: Harper and Row, 1969), 198.

6. Jean Norton Cru, *Témoins* (Paris: les Etincelles, 1929. [reprinted Nancy: presses universitaires, 1993]), 28.

7. Grant, *The Personal Memoirs of U. S. Grant*, 179.

8. The authenticity and context of the "humbugged" quote is discussed in Longford, *Wellington, The Years of the Sword*, 421. Humbugged does not mean surprised, it means deceived or hoaxed.

9. On May 12, 1815, he wrote to his brother Henry that although "There has been a good deal of movement upon the frontier in the last week, but I am inclined to believe it is entirely defensive, and that Buonaparte cannot venture to quit Paris," while on June 13th, he wrote Lord Lyndoch that Napoleon's departure from Paris was "not likely to be immediate. We are too strong for him here"; see *Dispatches of Field-Marshal the Duke of Wellington*, edited Walter Wood (London: Grant and Richards, 1902), 434–435. But notice Wellington's turn of phrase: "I am inclined to believe" is hardly the same thing as saying "I don't believe," or "there is no chance." Although Grant's mastery of the written word is justly and universally acclaimed, his sentences are rarely parsed. In the quote above, for instance, the word "apprehension" is routinely scanned as being synonymous with certainty, but it is in no way the same as saying "I know" or "I am convinced." On the contrary, the primary sense of the word is as it was historically in the English language, when it meant fear or anxiety.

10. William Preston Johnston, *The Life of General Albert Sidney Johnston* (New York: Appleton and Crofts, 1878) 452.

Chapter 8 Notes

1. Ulysses S. Grant, *The Personal Memoirs of U. S. Grant*, edited E. B. Long (New York: Da Capo Press, 1982), 193.

2. Grant, *The Personal Memoirs of U. S. Grant*, 197.

3. Halleck "not only threw away most of the advantages gained for him by his subordinates, but . . . so scattered his army that little was accomplished for six months." J. F. C. Fuller, *The Generalship of Ulysses S. Grant* (New York: Da Capo Press, 1991), 118.

4. First quote from Fuller, *Generalship of Grant*, 169; second quote from General James Marshall-Cornwall's excellent account, *Grant as Military Commander* (London: B. T. Batsford, 1970), 87.

5. Grant, *The Personal Memoirs of U. S. Grant*, 211.

Chapter 9 Notes

1. Ulysses S. Grant, *The Personal Memoirs of U. S. Grant*, edited E. B. Long (New York: Da Capo Press, 1982), 274.

2. See the account in Sylvanus Cadwallader, *Three Years with Grant,* edited Benjam P. Thomas (Lincoln: University of Nebraska Press, 1955), 91–92. Grant's idea was that the moment an assault was seen to be on the verge of failure, it should be halted. The heavy casualties in this and later assaults were incurred by men like McClernand; in this case in an attempt to boost his reputation. Fortunately, in June, Grant was able to have the man removed from command, basing his order on a technical violation of war department rules.
3. Grant, *The Personal Memoirs of U. S. Grant,* 277.
4. A famous letter; most of it is to be found in James Marshall-Cornwall, *Grant as Military Commander* (London: B. T. Batsford, 1970), 118.

Chapter 10 Notes

1. As recorded by John Russell Young, *Around the World with General Grant,* edited Michael Fellman (Baltimore: Johns Hopkins University Press, 2002), 384.
2. The British general James Marshall-Cornwall, who distinguished himself in two world wars and went on to write one of the very best accounts of Grant's generalship, puts it this way in *Grant as Military Commander* (London: B. T. Batsford, 1970): "Had Grant been allowed to carry out this perfectly feasible operation, he would have tightened the Union stranglehold on the Confederate economy and possibly shortened the war by a year" (118). Not to mention the fact that this strategy would also have meant less fighting and hence fewer losses.
3. Ulysses S. Grant, *The Personal Memoirs of U. S. Grant,* edited E. B. Long (New York: Da Capo Press, 1982), 340.

Chapter 11 Notes

1. William L. Barney's invaluable short guide to the period, *Battleground for the Union* (Englewood Cliffs, New Jersey: Prentice-Hall, 1990), 218. Barney probably understates the case.
2. Marshall-Cornwall, a staff officer himself, argues the case based on the proximity of Grant's physical headquarters to Meade's; in other words, Grant did not trust Meade to operate independently, as he did Sherman and Thomas.
3. James Marshall-Cornwall, *Grant as Military Commander* (London: B. T. Batsford, 1970), 136. Grant was so desperate he offered a combat command to Buell, but that worthy declined, as it would mean serving under Sherman— the sort of attitude that gives the lie to apologies for his earlier behavior.
4. A good example of the fatuousness of much Civil War battle scorings of wins and losses. The psychological problems are described admirably in an essay prepared by A. Wilson Green (staff historian for Fredericksburg and Spotsylvania National Military Park). A version of it may be found at www.nps.gov/frsp/wshist.htm.

5. Horace Porter, *Campaigning with Grant*, edited Wayne C. Temple (New York: Bonanza Books, 1961), 69–70. Porter does not identify the general as Meade, but James Marshall-Cornwall, *Grant as Military Commander* (London: B. T. Batsford, 1970) does (153).
6. These figures have to be used with extreme caution. Thomas L. Livermore, in *Numbers and Losses in the Civil War in America* (Bloomington: University of Indiana Press, 1957), refused to give Confederate losses for these final battles. All we really have to go on is the numbers of Confederate prisoners taken (4,000 at Spotsylvania alone) and the final muster taken when Lee surrendered (at that point he had roughly 28,000 men).
7. Ulysses S. Grant, *The Personal Memoirs of U. S. Grant*, edited E. B. Long (New York: Da Capo Press, 1982), 434. In Marshall-Cornwall, *Grant as Military Commander*, this passage is cited rather contemptuously, as part of his critique of Grant's handling of the campaign (164). The evidence is entirely unconvincing: if so and so had happened, Lee would have been decisively beaten. As we discussed earlier, this line of reasoning cuts both ways. It also ignores a very basic fact: Lee was not going to be beaten in the field in one battle. He was made of sterner stuff, as was Grant. The word *choice* is important. Grant didn't say Lee was defeated, or beaten, he said "whipped" which in the usage of the time meant something quite different; broken in spirit might be a more precise expression nowadays.
8. Sylvanus Cadwallader, *Three Years with Grant*, edited Benjam P. Thomas (Lincoln: University of Nebraska Press, 1955), 181–182. This brief account is the single best example of Grant's effect on the men who served under him.

Chapter 12 Notes

1. As usual, Grant's observation that he was more concerned about Joseph Johnston than about Lee gets to the heart of the matter. "I never ranked Lee as high as some others of the army . . . that is to say, I never had as much anxiety when he was at my front as when Joe Johnston was in front," as recorded by John Russell Young, *Around the World with General Grant*, edited Michael Fellman (Baltimore: Johns Hopkins University Press, 2002), 384. The key phrase is "as high as . . . ."—Johnston is simply an example.
2. As reported by [Colonel] Bernard Serrigny, *Trente ans avec Pétain* (Paris: Plon, 1959), 56.
3. As recounted by Young, *Around the World with General Grant*, 330. Young's recording of Grant's musing on military matters is the only record we have of his views.
4. The entire dispatch is quoted in *Memoirs*, 223. Marshall-Cornwall rightly calls this "a model of what an operation directive should be, leaving the details planning . . . to the soldier and sailor on the spot," James Marshall-Cornwall, *Grant as Military Commander* (London: B. T. Batsford, 1970), 102.

5. Cited earlier, in a different context. See Horace Porter, *Campaigning with Grant,* edited Wayne C. Temple (New York: Bonanza Books, 1961), 373.

6. J. F. C. Fuller's discussion on casualties in *The Generalship of Ulysses S. Grant* (New York: Da Capo Press, 1991) (367–372) may be supplemented by more recent works, including his brief discussion in *Grant and Lee* (Bloomington: Indiana University Press, 1957), 242–284, and the Appendix (285). The most comprehensive rebuttal of these matters is found in Edward Bonekemper, *A Victor Not a Butcher, Grant's Overlooked Military Genius* (Washington, D.C.: Regnery, 2004). To a certain extent, such estimates, following Fuller's sharply negative judgment, posit a most unfavorable view of Lee, as in John D. McKenzie, *Uncertain Glory: Lee's Generalship Re-Examined* (New York: Hippocrene, 1997). I disagree with this approach. Lee was a world-class general; he simply wasn't Grant.

7. The remarks are of acute interest, as he was writing to Marshal Beresford, and was thus speaking as one professional soldier to another. The letter, written on July 4, 1815, is found in *Dispatches of Field-Marshal the Duke of Wellington,* edited Walter Wood (London: Grant and Richards, 1902), 459. The whole issue of tactical innovation, which derives from Fuller, is grossly over-emphasized.

8. The three historians, John Keegan, J. F. C. Fuller, and James Marshall-Cornwall, have all been cited in these notes. Two of the three were distinguished British officers and the first two are inarguably two of the last century's greatest military historians: their judgments should be taken carefully. It is an interesting fact, however, that their estimates of Grant's generalship, like mine, are substantially higher than those of his biographers, who seem to go out of their way to find fault with him. And since few if any recent accounts of the war deal comprehensively with military matters (despite their claims), it is hard to fix any real appreciation of Grant as a general.

9. As quoted by John G. Wilson, *General Grant* (New York: Appleton, 1913), 367.

10. "Among us the conduct of the war for these last fourteen months has been characterized by an absolute absence of coordination, General Joffre, General Sarrail, the minister of war, of the navy, each works in his own sphere without a higher direction or even a common goal," Charles Dupuis wrote to the president of France in October 1916. Substitute the names, and this could be the Confederacy. Letter reproduced in Serrigny, *Trente ans avec Pétain,* 129.

11. A remark made to me by a young army captain while we were taking the bus out to the airplane at Charles de Gaulle airport on June 6, 2004.

12. Colonel Preston Brown to the French general André Degoutte, as quoted by Robert Asprey, *At Belleau Wood* (New York: Putnams's sons, 1965) 100.

Chapter 13 Notes

1. Two recent studies by respected historians give scathing portraits of Wilson's mishandling of foreign affairs: Thomas Fleming, *The Illusion of Victory* (New

York: Basic Books, 2003) and Jim Powell, *Wilson's War* (New York: Crown Forum, 2005). There is an excellent and favorable assessment of Grant's presidency in Josiah Bunting III, *Ulysses S. Grant*, part of the American Presidents series presided over by Arthur Schlesinger, Jr.

Index

von Blücher, Gebhard, 158
Bolivar, Tennessee, 119
Bonaparte, Napoleon, 2, 12, 15, 64, 72,
    90, 96, 107, 158
    maxims of, 2, 24,72, 81, 93, 95, 96,
    156
    portrait of, 93
Borodino, 157
Bragg, Braxton, 91, 116, 139, 140, 142
Breckinridge, J. C., 92
Buchanan, James, 69, 168
Buckner, Simon Bolivar, 64
Buell, Don Carlos, 57, 62, 80, 96, 100,
    116. 155
Bull Run, First, (Manassas, Virginia),
    54, 56
Bull Run, Second (Manassas, Virginia),
    116
Burnside, Ambrose, 126, 140, 155

Cadwallader, Sylvanus, 153
Carnifax Ferry, Virginia, 54
Caesar, Julius, 12
cavalry, 16, 53–54, 69
cavalry charges, 53–54, 62
cavalry raids, 117, 119, 125, 128
censorship, lack of, 104
Champion Hill (Champion's
    Hill),Mississippi, 129–130
Chancellorsville, Virginia, 130
Charles, Archduke of Austria, 158
Chattanooga, 139, 140, 147
    battle of, 140–143
Chickamauga, Tennessee, 119, 139
Chickasaw Bayou, Mississippi, 125
Churchill, Winston, 13, 56
Clausewitz, Karl von, 10
Cold Harbor, Virginia, 153
Columbus, Ohio, 52
Confederacy
    advantages of in war, 41–42, 49
    basic reasons for defeat, 54
Corinth, Mississippi, 76, 99, 114, 119
    battle of, 116–117

Crimean War, 39, 75
Crittenden, Thomas, 92
Crump's Landing, Tennessee, 89, 94
Cumberland River, 38, 52, 59, 61, 65,
    66, 70, 75, 85, 139

Davis, Jefferson, 155, 156, 164, 165
Democratic Party, 3, 149
Dent, Julia, 17, 25
Department of Justice, 172
Department of the Gulf, 130
Department of the Mississippi, 83, 150
Department of the Missouri, 60, 83
Department of the Ohio, 83
Department of the Tennessee, 120
Department of the West, 51–52
Dieppe Raid, 56
Donelson, Fort, 59
    battles for, 67–68
    siege of, 65–66
    surrender of, 69
van Dorn, Earl. 117, 119
Dresden, 157
dysentery, 114

Eisenhower, Dwight D., 2, 137, 142,
    167
emancipation
    revoked by Lincoln, 60

first world war. See world war one
flank(s), 40, 91–92, 108, 110, 120, 129,
    130, 141, 142, 152
    Grant's preference for in attack, 36
    Idea of flank attacks not new, 141
    Prussian (German) preference for in
    battle, 162
Floyd, John, 65, 69
Foote, Andrew Hull, 62
Forrest, Nathan Bedford, 69, 125
forts, obsolescence of, 38
Franco-Prussian War, 79, 138
Frederick the Great, 118, 167
    tactical innovations of, 31

Fredericksburg, Maryland, 126, 140
Fremont, John C., 51
  strategic thinking, 52
  removal by Lincoln, 60, 76
French army: see army, French
frontal attacks, 34, 37, 163
Fuller, J. F. C., 93, 162

German army. See, army, German
Gettysburg, Pennsylvania, 37, 119, 133,
  139, 164
Grand Gulf, Mississippi, 128
Grant, Ulysses
  ability to visualize terrain, 160
  academic background, 9, 11
  aphorisms, 35, 161
  appointed commander-in-chief, 148
  attempts to resign, 114
  biographers and, 10
  birth and childhood, 8–9
  compared with Npoleon, 158
  compassion for wounded, 21
  confidence as commander, 166
  courtship and marriage, 17, 25, 28
  delegation of authority, 164
  difficulties of biographers with, 159
  emphasis on speed, 163
  encyclopedic knowledge of warfare,
  160, 164
  excellence in writing, 161
  financial crisis of 1873, 171
  flaws, 71, 160
  instincts, 43, 64
  mathematical abilities, 13
  memoirs, 20, 49, 51, 91, 106, 109,
  111, 112, 117, 130, 131, 143,
  160
  negative opinions of, 101–102
  overblown accounts of failure, 28
  penchant for secrecy, 127
  physical appearance, 8
  plans, 143, 151
  promotions after 1861, 139, 148
  Quartermaster in Mexican War, 21

rapid promotions, 27, 50, 51
reading, 15
regrets at enlisting, 20
removed from command, 111
reputation as a butcher, 97, 100
resigns commission, 26
reticence about experiences, 34
scandals during presidency, 170
skepticism of theory, 33
strengths in battle, 58
tactics, 36, 162
understanding of men, 163
unmilitary bearing, 22
West Point, 11, 164
worries, 112
Grierson, Benjamin, 128

Halleck, Henry, 57, 60, 101, 126, 130,
  138, 149, 169
  becomes commander-in-chief, 114
  careerism, 78
  intellectual abilities
  lack of understanding of warfare,
  115
  mistakes, 78, 113, 124, 158
  schemes against Grant, 75, 83
Hamburg Landing, Tennessee, 111
Harper's Weekly, 53, 56, 82, 101, 106,
  107
Harris, Thomas, 50
Hardee, William, 142
Heiman, Adolphus, 64
Heiman, Fort, 59
  abandonment of, 64
Henry, Fort, 59
  surrender of, 64
Hindman, Fort, 126
Hitchcock, Ethan Allen, 70
Hitler, 13
Holly Springs, Mississippi, 119, 125
Hood, John, 154, 155
Hooker, Joseph
Humboldt, Tennessee, 125, 128
Hurlbut, Stephen A., 119